Bush Aussies

Allan Nixon is a bushie. He was born in an old Victorian mining town and now lives at the base of a mountain range north of Melbourne. Known as 'The Uteman' as a result of his bestselling *Beaut Utes* series of books, Allan travels around Australia writing and gathering material for future works. His writing and photography has featured in numerous newspapers and magazines, including *Outback* magazine. *Bush Aussies* is his eighteenth book.

Other Books by Allan M. Nixon:

Bush Aussies

ALLAN M. NIXON, 'THE UTEMAN'

VIKING
an imprint of
PENGUIN BOOKS

PENGUIN BOOKS

Published by the Penguin Group
Penguin Group (Australia)
250 Camberwell Road, Camberwell, Victoria 3124, Australia
(a division of Pearson Australia Group Pty Ltd)
Penguin Group (USA) Inc.
375 Hudson Street, New York, New York 10014, USA
Penguin Group (Canada)
90 Eglinton Avenue East, Suite 700, Toronto, Canada ON M4P 2Y3
(a division of Pearson Penguin Canada Inc.)
Penguin Books Ltd
80 Strand, London WC2R 0RL England
Penguin Ireland
25 St Stephen's Green, Dublin 2, Ireland
(a division of Penguin Books Ltd)
Penguin Books India Pvt Ltd
11 Community Centre, Panchsheel Park, New Delhi – 110 017, India
Penguin Group (NZ)
67 Apollo Drive, Rosedale, North Shore 0632, New Zealand
(a division of Pearson New Zealand Ltd)
Penguin Books (South Africa) (Pty) Ltd
24 Sturdee Avenue, Rosebank, Johannesburg 2196, South Africa

Penguin Books Ltd, Registered Offices: 80 Strand, London, WC2R 0RL, England

First published by Penguin Group (Australia), 2007

1 3 5 7 9 10 8 6 4 2

Cover and text design by Karen Trump © Penguin Group (Australia)
Cover photographs by Bill Bachmann and Australian Scenics
Photograph on p. 88 by Matthew Newton
Photograph on p. 193 by David Oldfield
Typeset in 12.5/17.8 pt Aldus by Post Pre-press Group, Brisbane, Queensland
Printed and bound in Australia by McPherson's Printing Group, Maryborough, Victoria

National Library of Australia
Cataloguing-in-Publication data:

Nixon, Allan M., 1951– .
Bush Aussies.
ISBN 9780670071449 (pbk.).
1. Country life – Australia – Social life and customs. 2. Australia – Biography.
3. Australia – Rural conditions. I. Title.

920.094

penguin.com.au

To Graham Williams (1953–2004),
a computer whizz, who always kept mine going,
a talented builder, who did so much to my home,
and a great bloke.
You left your mark on the world, mate.

Acknowledgements

I would like to thank a number of people for helping to make this book a reality. Thank you to all the people who cooperated in having their story told and who allowed me into their homes and workplaces.

At Penguin Books: sincere thanks to my publisher, Ali Watts, for her usual professional and friendly support. Special thanks to my editor, Bridget Maidment (our first book together), and my designer, Karen Trump (daughter of a bush beekeeper). Both are easy to work with, and I'm grateful for their talents; they made my job easier.

Thanks to my family for their ongoing interest and support, especially Janette, who puts up with my comings and goings and constant changes to my schedules.

Thanks to Dusty for the great 'welcome home' I get every time I come back.

Contents

Introduction

'TO A PERSON WITH IMAGINATION, A MAP IS THE
WINDOW TO ADVENTURE.'
SIR FRANCIS CHICHESTER

People often ask me how I find the characters who make it into the pages of my books. Well, if you don't like driving, you wouldn't like my job because I do a lot of travelling in search of what I want. I spend many hours looking over maps just reading places names and researching the history of areas. I was in my office very early one morning – about 2 a.m. – looking over my maps, and I saw the wonderful name 'Chinkapook'. It's a town in Victoria, and I couldn't remember if I'd ever been there. That was enough of a reason for me to go visit the place. The writer in me came out and I thought of a chapter titled 'Chinkapook Charlie' – I thought it had a nice-sounding ring to it. Next day I was off bright and early to check out the character of the town, and the people who live there. I never did find a Chinkapook Charlie, but I did get a good story in a town nearby. I still hope I might come across a Chinkapook Charlie one day.

Not all my stories are red herrings or dead ends or come out on the spur of the moment, even though those sorts of stories are fun to do anyway. Often I'll hear a whisper from someone who knew all about the life of some bloke who 'lives somewhere in mid-New South Wales, and I don't know his name, but someone at the pub at Wyalong might know him'. That's enough for me to start delving, if I think it could be a good story. People also write letters to me with details of interesting characters, or I pull out scraps of newspaper articles about people and add them to my huge collection of 'possible stories'. With one bloke, I hung on to a newspaper clipping for years before I finally tracked him down – he's in this book.

I've driven thousands of kilometres in the hope I'd get a particular story; I've been told that people weren't interested, but then sat down with them only to have them tell me everything. If you show people you're genuinely interested in their story, they're usually very pleased. I don't mind how long it takes to get someone's story so long as they keep the cuppas coming. I once sat up on a verandah roof, interviewing a man while he replaced the iron on the roof. Once a bloke in Alice Springs got me so drunk while he was telling me his story that he had to drive me home – I could hardly walk! The lesson is: never try to out-drink or even keep up with an ex-cattle drover. They are thirsty men. Now I try to avoid writing over a beer. I don't know how Henry Lawson did it.

There's one thing this book proves – there's a lot of Bush Aussies who are really talented and haven't let being isolated from cities stop them from working their jobs, doing their thing and living the life they want. In these pages you will meet some people who live miles down a dusty country road, but whose businesses take them all over the world. Cody and Sarah train animals for movies and their international business is very successful, as is Karen's. She does decorative work in mansions and castles alike in wherever her work takes her.

There are those who are content to simply enjoy life in the bush. No longer are people tied to the city to make a living; many people now do their jobs from home with their head office in a major city many miles away. Today's technology allows us more freedom than ever. I wrote many of my stories sitting in my ute under a gum tree by a river, or in the outback, or in a caravan park, or in a main street café, or in my office at home, or God knows where on the road.

The people in this book live in country towns and properties ranging from many thousands of acres to small patches of dirt. Sparra gets around by horse and cart, while Bev and Laurie travel the country in their mobile home.

The people here are in the main unsung, they are the ordinary everyday bloke or sheila from the bush. They are wonderful in their own unique ways. They are the *Bush Aussies*.

If you know of an interesting character you'd like me to interview, please contact me c/o PO Box 46, Essendon North, Victoria 3041.

Allan 'The Uteman' Nixon
Swagman's Rest
June 2007

Water Diviner

JACK McMAHON

'WITH DRILLING, NO TWO HOLES ARE THE SAME,
AND NO TWO SITES ARE THE SAME.'

Jack McMahon would be the first to say he's seen quite a bit of life. He is a very well read man and is full of stories. 'There's no life without books,' he says. He left school after failing Year Nine but has seen and done much in his seventy years. His father, Jack, was a gold miner and his mother, Edith, had family who were also miners.

His wife, Loreto, says she knew when Jack came home after a day's work what sort of mood he would be in. She'd look out the window to see how much pipe casing was still on the ute – if there wasn't much, then she knew he'd drilled deep that day. 'Also if there was mud on his boots and pants, I'd know it was a good day's work. No mud meant no money,' she says casually. 'Water drilling can be extraordinarily stressful: all that expensive equipment, pipes and gear underground that could break. You need a lot of patience, but it's also very exhilarating.'

Loreto met Jack in a pub. 'I was going out with someone else at the time and he came out of the pub and said, "I want you to meet a bloke." It was Jack. A couple of weeks later I received a letter from Jack, and six weeks later we were married. My friends all said not to marry him. He had a terrible reputation – he's a driller and a drinker.'

Jack laughs. 'We all were.'

After forty years of marriage, two sons and many ups and downs, Jack and Loreto are still together, retired in their home in the bush and living life the way they enjoy.

Their eldest son, John, has a baby, Lucy, with Talya; while younger son, Dan, is now running the business that Jack started – Centre State Drilling. Three dogs keep them occupied and Jack is in the middle of building a new site to grow hydroponics. A backhoe was clearing the side of a hill on their 50 acres the day I arrived. It was Jack's seventieth birthday.

Penny the cocker spaniel and Lena and Zeus the rottweilers were all excited, and Jack warned me to be a bit careful. However, dogs know whether you are a dog lover or not, and it wasn't long before I was being licked and greeted as a long lost friend. 'I've never known Lena to take to someone like that before,' says Jack.

I've always had a good time with dogs; they soon figure out that I love them with a passion. They are much smarter than we give them credit for.

You know instantly when you start talking to Jack that he has a million stories to tell. He is writing his own book in his spare time. As he talks, he casually mentions in conversation his past jobs and the list grows and grows. What is here is but a snippet of the life of Jack.

Loreto sums up their life so far. 'We've had forty-one very interesting, fulfilling years with lots of ups and downs. I never wanted to live an ordinary life.'

With Jack it could never be boring. I wanted to learn more about where it all began.

'I left school at fourteen, and worked as a grocer's assistant for three months. Later I worked as a counter jumper in an electrical shop, but I lit a cigarette out the back of the shop in the battery room and blew it up, blew it to bits, so I was sacked,' he laughs loudly. 'Then I went wood cutting and truck driving and later worked for an agricultural place driving, and then finally ended up in the McAllister River country near Licola in Gippsland for about three or five years driving timber trucks and dozers as well as doing a bit of timber felling.'

I soon learnt that dates and years aren't Jack's strongest memories. 'I then went earthmoving in about 1958–59.'

'We were all piss-heads, the whole lot of us, all running from someone or something,' he says matter-of-factly. 'I drifted about a lot, worked for State Rivers at one stage, but the less said about them the better. Then in the 1960s, when work was easy to get, I ended up as a driller, auto-electrician and dozer driver on the Snowy Mountains Scheme. I turned my hand to anything. I even worked in a car-yard in Melbourne for a while once. Anyway I worked on the Snowy and was at Geehi for over twelve months. There are too many yarns up there to go into, if you get what I mean. I was there over three years alto-gether and saw a lot.'

I asked Jack if the stories I'd heard of unexplained deaths on the Snowy were true. We talked for a while about it, but the mysteries surrounding it won't be dealt with here.

'It was hard work, no question of that. It was like

a production line, but there was no regard for safety, it was all drive, drive, drive. I had lots of yarns and saw lots. It was a common effort, though, and it was marvellous to see all the nationalities come together. Initially they had separate camps for different nationalities, but then they chucked us all in together, and one boss said, "We'll use the survivors." Anyway they had to get on together. There were even seventeen or eighteen German ex-SS people there, but they broke them up. Germans pretending to be Austrians, and all that sort of stuff.'

Jack then went back to the timber country for a while, and starting laying pipeline. 'I was in the grip of the piss well and truly by then,' he says straightforwardly. 'Drink became the master until one day I finally said, "That's enough."' He hasn't had a drink now in over thirty years.

He does remember one incident that he laughs about now, but at the time it was very serious.

'I was working with other men 70 miles from the nearest pub, so we built a new still and soon had plenty of whisky to drink. However, somehow the customs and excise people got onto us. My lawyer said they were "after my arse". You can't do the government out of their money. I had been a beekeeper at one stage up near Underbool, so I said to my lawyer that I was going to use the excuse that I was using the still to distil water for the bees. He said I wouldn't get away with it.

'When we got to court I used it as my excuse. The magistrate was okay, but when the prosecutor could see it was going our way he jumped up and said, "We demand a pecuniary penalty." The old beak put him in his place by saying, "In my court you don't demand anything – you respectfully request it."

'Anyway, then the prosecutor tried to use precedence of a case against some other people, but the judge said that they

weren't Australian citizens. Anyway the old judge looked down at the clerk of courts and said, "What is the pecuniary penalty?" He then fined me $130 and I became the first Australian-born citizen to be charged with building and using a whisky still.'

Jack briefly mentions some other jobs he's had, like plant fitter, egg truck driver, a turner at Thompsons Foundry, a chainsaw operator and road maintenance worker with the Forest Commission, the most boring job he ever held. He also did national service in 1956 in the air force.

'Later I was bridge-building and laying pipelines, but never on scrapers – they are the widow makers of the earthmoving business. I drove bulldozers and end dumpers or belly dumpers and was also doing some drilling which is always the biggest challenge.'

Jack worked on the building of Lake Eppalock driving an International BD24 bulldozer. He remembers it as being 'state of the art of the time'.

In the 1960s Jack lost an eye in a car accident. 'We were pissed and playing cards with mates in a pub in Melbourne. I'd won between £200 and £300. I bought a Rolex watch. About 3 a.m. we headed back to the motel. I told my mate to watch his driving, and sure enough there were truck lights in the window one minute, and the next thing I knew I woke up in hospital – it was a month later. My mate wrote off a brand new Holden and escaped with a cut finger, but I was in a bad way. There is one funny thing, though: the bloke that caused the accident was thrown clear but scraped off both his testicles on the roadway. Not funny for him, I guess.'

So how did Jack find out he could divine water? 'I was about seven or eight years old. An old bloke, "Davey" Davenport, was a beekeeper who drove an old A-model ute. He was a funny old bloke – a small man who was hit in the face when his gun blew up. Half his nose was missing. One hot day I saw him down a hole. I thought he was digging for gold. He said that he was digging a well for water. I asked how he knew he'd find water by digging there. He showed me how to with a piece of fencing wire and I couldn't believe it. When I told my dad he said that it was all bullshit, that only charlatans and rogues did it. Dad never lived to see me become a water diviner or driller – he'd have been horrified. Anyway I soon forgot about it and didn't think about it again for years.

'Anyway, later it became very much an integral part of my business. It works for me; I don't give a shit if it doesn't work for others. You know, the Chinese were doing it 6000 years ago, and it was accepted over many centuries in all sorts of societies. Metaphysics is the next frontier. Quantum mechanics and all that. I had to do a lot of reading on it all, and you have to know it – it's your business. The English are the best at water divining. Germans were also good. T.C. Lethbridge, an Oxford don, a man of independent means with no axe to grind, wrote one of the best books on the subject. Some diviners are brilliant at what they do.

It was evident Jack had spent a lot of time reading about the ways of water divining – or dowsing, as the old term is.

'With drilling, no two holes are the same, and no two sites are the same. You always work ahead of the machine to try and see what is coming – sand, clay, rock, shale.'

Jack bought his first drilling rig, a cable rig, in 1982 or '83. 'I bought it off an old bloke. I got my driller's licence and have been at it ever since. Then I went on to rotary drilling. The first rigs were primitive. Mine would drill 30 or 40 feet on a good day and used 4 to 5 gallons of diesel in the old Southern Cross IG33 motor. You were very much in touch with the earth. At one stage I also did gold leases drilling with a sampling rig.

'By 1986 I knew what I wanted so I designed and built a compressed air rig with a rotary bit and hammer drill. It was a big bastard. I'd do 300 to 400 feet a day and use 200 gallons of diesel. Now our rig is a new custom-built rig, which drills about 400–500 feet a day.

'Over the years we've mainly done water-boring at places from Kinglake and Wallan in the east to St Arnaud in the west. Other places like Bendigo, Romsey, over central Victoria mainly. We did a lot of work in New South Wales at Coffs Harbour and Sawtell as well. They had permanent water restrictions there, and there was very good underground water there. People were making good money or had a bit, so I enjoyed working up there.

'Some people still don't believe it works,' he says. 'One old lady asked me to leave a job on her property as she said I was "in league with the devil",' he says with a great laugh.

'I always divined my holes on jobs. You have to pick the site with care because no water meant no pay. I haven't divined for three years now. I'm well and truly retired, and don't miss working. My son Dan runs the business and he's a brilliant water diviner, much better than I ever was. The business has been operating over fifty years now, and Dan has been involved for more than twenty years.'

So it was time to leave the three dogs, Loreto their Mum and Jack the great reader with his house full of books. Before I left, Jack showed me how he made the divining rod work. I had a go and I certainly felt something in my right hand through the wire, but other than that I couldn't get it to respond like Jack could.

I hope Jack writes his autobiography – it will make interesting reading. Although he has a million yarns Jack says, 'I've just lived an ordinary working-man's life.'

smiley

'WE MUST ALWAYS PLEASE THE BEER GODS.'

'They reckon I always smiled a lot. I've had a rough life, I suppose. I was born in 1940, but at four months old I was put into St Joseph's Babies Home and then Aidan Street Orphanage. I ran away twice and the second time I stayed away, but by then I was twenty-two.'

Smiley has a good view on life and often says, 'How lucky we are,' or, 'We should be thankful'. She knows what makes her happy in life – her dogs, geese, chooks and horses – and Aussie beer. 'We must always please the beer gods,' she says with a laugh. 'It's as good an excuse as any for having a beer.'

Smiley's husband died a few years ago; her five children are all grown up and she is proud grandmother to ten kids. She lives on Walton's Mountain in the bush, and life goes on.

It was a couple of days before the state election, and Smiley threw a question at me. 'Why do we have to sign ballot forms in pencil?' she asked. 'It's a legal document, yet we have to sign in pencil.' It was a question I couldn't answer, so I threw one back at her. How come we have seven Labor state governments and yet a Liberal federal one? Does that mean people change their votes? I've asked that of many people from all walks of life and no one can ever tell me the answer. The things you talk about over a good hot cuppa. Smiley put some nice hot scones straight from the oven on the table next to me.

Smiley is a good cook. She was taught well at the orphanage. 'The nuns were tough, but I guess they had to be – look what they had to do. They really set me up with life skills. They taught me everything – to cook, sew. I learnt how to make mattresses and pillows, and later I worked in the kitchen. Mother Antonio was a favourite; I worked in the kitchen with her – she's still alive; she came to my sixty-fifth birthday. I still see a lot of the girls I was in the orphanage with. They were my family.

'I was always in trouble at the orphanage: I often would climb out the window and go down to the lemon grove, but I'd be caught and then I had to stand in the corner as punishment. I found a little kitten once and kept it hidden up my jumper, but eventually it disappeared. I remember one of the priests owned greyhound dogs, and a friend and I were down in the yard one day and we saw the dogs and I said to her, "Oh look Mary, the poor things are so skinny, let's feed them good." Well, didn't we cop a hiding for that? The priest was training them for racing but we didn't know. He was furious, but we thought they just looked half starved. Our punishment for that was to stand barefoot in the kitchen slop cans. But we weren't too worried; I said to Mary, "Don't worry, our feet are warmer in here than out." '

But not everything in the orphanage was to her dislike. 'We had really good Christmases there,' Smiley remembers fondly.

'By the time I was six I'd learnt to master making the bed, all beautiful cast-iron beds. By the time I was fourteen I was working in the kitchen. There were a hundred people to cook for, including twenty-four nuns. Three girls worked in the scullery and the rest in the kitchen. I also learnt to make bread in the bake-house, as well as how to preserve fruit – and I'm still doing it.

'Finally I ran away again when I was twenty-two and didn't go back. I got to Melbourne and stayed with a friend for a while and then got a job at Fowlers Vacola doing bottling and peeling fruit in their factory. I had other jobs – at Dorf Taps and others. I met Frank at a party and thought I wouldn't like to marry him. He was so skinny and scrawny, I'd have to feed him so much.

'The orphanage didn't teach me everything, though. When I first went shopping in a store I ran out of money. You see, we always had things in bulk – big bags in the kitchen orphanage – so I bought big bags of flour, sugar, etc., but soon ran out of money. Frank said, "What have you done? There's enough food here to feed an army!" and I still hadn't bought everything we needed. He couldn't believe it!' Smiley laughs at the memory. 'And there were other things I didn't learn from the orphanage. Frank and I were invited to a function and I was told to "bring a plate". Well, I did – a whole dinner set! – and I was proud that I also brought knives and forks as well! I didn't know it meant bring a plate of food.

'Another time I went to a bloke's house and said, "You advertised a garage sale?" "Yep," he says. So I proceeded to ask,

"Is this it? Does it come with the doors?" I thought a garage sale meant you bought the garage, not a whole heap of junk in it.' Smiley again laughs her head off at her early days in the big, bad world outside of the orphanage.

'Anyway, Frank and I were married for forty-five years, and I had a few miscarriages, but five kids later we had a good life together. We helped a lot of handicapped kids. The majority of us are all selfish, but I think we should be thankful for how lucky we really are.

'Frank was a printer; we had our own business – Lincoln Press. Our eldest son Kerry John, forty, is a printer and consultant; Lydia Ann, thirty-nine, is a housewife; Dean Paul, thirty-eight, is a printer; then we had twins Alison Carmella, who works with disabled children, and Raquel Terese, a swimming instructor; the twins are thirty-six. I've ten grandchildren aged from eleven down to two years old.

'When Frank retired he was sick and that's when we bought the 20-acre farm. He knew I always wanted one as I have always loved animals. We are very, very lucky people, really. We worked hard all our lives, so we then had time to enjoy our hobby.'

The results of Frank and Smiley's hobby lie in the various sheds around Walton's Mountain. 'Frank went to buy a car for a friend, but ended up bringing it home instead. He didn't say much at first, though. He'd put some petrol in it and it started straight away. He wanted to buy it, so I said, "So long as it makes you happy," and that was the start of it. It was an old Clyno car. Finally, when we had ten old cars I put my foot down and said, "If one more car comes into this yard, that's it!"' Smiley has a good laugh and another sip of her tea.

'Would you believe one day I looked out the window and

there were a heap of teenagers down the back fence, and I asked Frank, "What are they up to?" He said, "Don't worry about them." What I didn't know was that he'd pulled a whole car to bits and got them to carry it in bits through the bush, over the fence and into the shed so I wouldn't see another car in the place. Finally we had Clyno cars and utes – models for 1922, '23, '24, '25, '26 and '27, a Rolls Royce, two Buicks, a Chevrolet, a Pontiac, a Vanguard, a couple of Morris Minors, a Holden FJ ute and a Chev truck.'

Now, before all you car collectors start drooling and looking for Smiley's address, don't bother – the Rolls Royce has already gone to one of the daughters, and the rest of the vehicles are all spoken for by other members of the family. And besides, if they weren't, I'd have my own hand up for the old utes. Thankfully though, Smiley's family have a good appreciation of their parents' restored vehicles.

'We had a lot of fun with the vehicles; we always took the kids away with us on rallies and trips. We went to Tasmania once. Our vehicles have appeared in numerous movies and TV shows over the years – things like *Power Without Glory*, *On the Waterfront* and *Carson's Law*.

'We had our arguments over them. I remember we'd worked all afternoon on one, taped it all up ready for painting. I made tea and called to Frank to come in before his tea got cold. He ignored me and continued working, so I went out and pulled all the tape off that I'd spent hours putting on. He was never late for tea again.'

Smiley still uses the FJ Holden ute. Neighbours rely on it, too. It has been made into a one-tonne tray-top ute with water tank. 'That's my fire-truck,' says Smiley. 'Some of the neighbours get water carried in it as well.'

Smiley could never be lonely on Walton's Mountain. She has Porkey's Bar to occupy her – a shed devoted to a large collection of beer cars, with room for billiard table, bar, dart board, fridge full of home brew and shop-bought beer, and a lounge for friends and family. 'I love my darts,' she says. 'I'm still a member of two darts associations.'

Smiley has her own orchard now, just like when she was at the orphanage. 'I have orange, apricot, peach, pear, apple and nectarine trees. I do my own preserving. One of my grandkids said to me one day, "Why don't you go down the street everyday to do shopping?" I said to go look in the pantry – when he came back after seeing all my preserves jars and homegrown stuff he said, "Boy, Gran, you won't have to go down the street for a whole year!" I also have chooks and geese and pigs. I don't eat the animals I give a name to, so they are all called "Freezer" at one time or another. I've got three horses – April, Maggie May and Ward junior. The dogs are Lucky, fifteen (he was a pound dog) and Monty, eight. The cat I call Black Douglas after the drink.'

About fifteen years ago Smiley found her real mother. 'I'd been looking for many years, and when I finally went to see her we got on okay. She said she was expecting me to come one day. I was amazed she had the same things as me – crochet tablecloths and many other items I also had. It was unreal. Mum has worked hard all her life. She was in the Land Army. I don't know anything about my father. My mum's eighty-five now and in respite care, and she sees the rest of the family. Someone asked me one day, "You're not bitter?" My answer is, why should I be? I can't change it, and I won't hassle my mother about it. She said, "You and I will do okay. Just don't ask too many questions," and so I don't.

'I was always a bit of a villain actually. I've always managed to get into trouble, but I always get out of it. My number in the orphanage was twenty-three, I still use it on my Tattslotto form. I've done lots of things that I wanted to over the years. I've played my guitar and sung at Tamworth, busked in Peel Street and yodelled in the RSL and in pubs. I've done tabletop dancing in a pub; I've played football and cricket; I've done part-time jillaroo work; I've printed magazines and learnt to bind books. I love my country music, especially Reg Lindsay, Slim Whiteman and Slim Dusty. I learnt to do line dancing and boot-scooting. I remember coming home drunk with friends and we followed the white line in the centre of the road to get home and danced as we went. I've been a chronic asthmatic and I've got a heart problem. I lost the use of one eye, which is hereditary, but life goes on.'

Smiley and I wandered around the yard, patting horses and dogs and looking at the view down the valley. I loved her vintage vehicles covered in dust, just waiting to spring into life again. It was late afternoon and time for me to head south.

I wanted one last quote from her to pass on to readers.

'Always put your children first, and to them I hope that they achieve what they want, but they have to work hard at it.'

I'll raise a glass to the beer gods on that one, Smiley.

Discover Dingoes

LYN & PETER WATSON

'UNTIL YOU OWN A DINGO, YOU KNOW NOTHING ABOUT DOGS.'

Before I start this story, I must first confess to being a total supporter of the dingo (and dogs in general), and I believe they need to be fully recognised across Australia as a unique and important part of the natural world.

In my job, where I travel thousands of kilometres all over Australia chasing interviews, taking photographs and just loving the travel, I have seen many dingoes in the remotest parts of the outback. I have sat and watched them hunting or playing. Most, though, were solitary wanderers and very wary of getting too close. I have seen them in captivity, seen them as pets and know of people who'd shoot them on sight. People seem to either love or hate dingoes. I also know some pretty special dingoes like Dinky the Singing Dingo south of Alice Springs, and Ernie the dingo from near Moomba, who has his own business card and is employed to hunt and 'tree' wild cats as part of a research program.

Little did I know that not far away a group of dingoes were having a house and property left to them in a will to ensure their ongoing survival and breeding. I didn't have far to drive to see them.

Years ago I interviewed Bruce Jacobs, 'Australia's dingo man', famous for his many years of work breeding dingoes. He was also famous for the stoushes he had with the then Department of Conservation, Forests and Lands and with the Victorian RSPCA, led by Dr Hugh Worth. The media had a field day when the authorities raided his property and either shot or took his dingoes. A long court case followed, and Bruce finally had his dingoes returned to him, much to the chagrin of the authorities. He also received a compensation package. Much fencing was supplied so long as he didn't sue. Government departments call it 'shut-up money'.

I sat with Bruce on a log as he rolled a ciggie. We were surrounded by his family of dingoes, and you soon learned how much he loved them and they loved him. Sadly, when he died his dingo farm was broken up and again he made the headlines. I went to his funeral, and along with many other dingo lovers. I was there to remember the man who had given his life to the dingo. Bruce had done a great deal in his life to make the world aware of the native dog. Media from all over the world came to his farm to see the dogs, and he spent a great deal of time promoting them; Bruce wanted to see the purity of the dingo maintained, and he worked with numerous scientists looking at the genetics of the dogs.

Now others work in the promotion of dingoes, and they have acted sooner rather than later to ensure their work will live on after they too are gone. Lyn and Peter Watson operate the Dingo Discovery Centre. Lyn knew Bruce Jacobs long before he had his dingoes, back when he bred afghan hounds. Bruce's story can be read in my book *Beaut Utes* in a chapter titled 'Fifteen dead emus, ninety howling dingoes, three barking dogs . . . & a Holden Rodeo'.

'I got Peter at the kennel club,' says Lyn with a laugh. No, she didn't buy him or put a collar on him, but she did meet him because of their shared love of dogs. Peter was the first elected president of the KCC (now the Victorian Canine Association) and one of his claims to fame is that while he was president, and after a lot of hard work, he got the Australian dingo recognised as a breed. His big aim now is to see them recognised as a separate species.

'Charles Darwin got it right,' says Peter. 'He called them *Canis dingo*. Not *Canis familiarus dingo*. He recognised it as a separate species.'

You can usually tell a bit about people by what's in their house. Lyn and Peter leave not a doubt. When I pulled up in the driveway of their home a large scottish deerhound came to greet me and gave me a big, wet, slobbering kiss. We walked to the front door, past two bronze statues of dingoes, and further across the garden was a large steel silhouette of a dingo. Inside, Lyn showed me the wonderful home she designed and built with Peter. The house is full of dog statues, and the walls are covered in framed dog and dingo limited edition pictures, as well as many other beautiful mementos they have collected from around the world.

Peter worked in India for eighteen months and he shipped home a container load of wonderful exotic statues and tables and such. A large engraved brass urn sits at the front of the house with water and floating flowers in it. Two large elephant carvings and other treasures welcome visitors, but the most amazing sight is through huge glass windows: a southerly view down the valley towards Melbourne. This is a home, not a house. The home is flanked on two sides by forest, making this a perfect environment not only for Lyn and Peter but the dingoes too. The first thing you see outside their gate back on the main road is a sign that says this is 'land for wildlife'. They are passionate about their dingoes, but they are also passionate about all wildlife and the natural environment. And they are prepared to put their money where their mouths are. A nankeen kestrel hovers on the wind near the home. Peter says they constantly have four eagles visiting them. There are many native grasses back on the property now; fifty to sixty kangaroos feed at night in the paddock and other birds come and go. Swamp wallabies, koalas, echidnas, and more all call this home. Magpies come and are fed off the verandah.

Because they are dingo breeders and keen to protect the animals, closed-circuit monitoring, electric fences and other security measures are all part of the deal.

Lyn and Peter showed me the documents the solicitors drew up to establish the Dingo Foundation. The home and land and 'anything dingo' will be left to the Foundation to carry on their work long after the Watsons have gone. This is to ensure the pure bred dingo lives on.

Lyn and Peter's 'Team Dingo' is being organised as an Internet resource to ensure that people the world over are made more aware of the dingo and its true role in the Australian ecological system. The website provides daily updates of anything happening in the dingo world. Bindi Irwin has been asked to be member number one.

The dingo holds a weird place in Australian history: it has been both loved and maligned. Governments confuse the issue more. In Queensland you can only have a dingo on permit *if* it is de-sexed, thus preventing any breeding. In South Australia and Tasmania they are banned outright. Western Australia is in limbo somewhere between having permits and being banned altogether. In the Northern Territory it is open for anyone to own a dingo; New South Wales and the ACT are both unregulated and it's okay to own a dingo. Victoria has a permit system. Seems politicians can't agree on the right way to go.

Dingoes are well recognised and appreciated overseas. The Dingo Foundation and Trust that the Watsons are setting up already includes some keen people like Mariko Hyland, a Japanese lady living in Australia; she also set up the Koala Trust. Frank Seymour, who runs the Quindalup Fauna Park, near Margaret River, Western Australia, is also a member. He's a nature specialist who even grows his own plankton. He is also involved with the designing of trails and water features, new shelters for the dingoes and education centres. He is also Lyn's brother.

Some of the sponsors include Olympian Bob Lay, a lady from Chicago, a vet from Illinois, and the president of the Western Australian Dingo Association. Bloodstock syndicator Shelley Hancox is another who sponsors one of Lyn and Peter's dingoes. Other people include volunteers who help out at the centre – young people interesting in ecology, students of zoology, a doctor, an admin officer for the CFA (Country Fire Authority), a computer whiz, a film maker, and many others. One dollar a day goes towards the feeding of the animals and they receive a certificate, a photo of the dog they sponsor and they can visit the dog as well.

I wanted to know which dingoes they had here at the moment. Between them, Peter and Lyn rattled off the names: Tom, nineteen, is one of the bosses; Paprika is sixteen; A.J. is nine, and a bossy alpha bitch; Teddy is described as a 'wolf of gold'; Jedda is one of three black dingoes, along with Stormy, a black from Western Australia and Clancy, a black from Griffith, New South Wales; Zombie is one of two whites from central New South Wales; Snowgum, another white; Yaouk was rescued from death row, and Coyote was also rescued; Djarrah was an orphan found in the wild and raised on marsupial replacement milk in Mt Isa; Wilka came from Currumbin Zoo in Queensland; Freckle is the most expensive, with a broken leg that has cost thousands to repair, and Lyn still works at the vet even now to pay it off. The others include Dottley, Cinnamon, Cinders and Snip. The final ones are the four to five month-old pups – Stirling, Opal, Bingo and Ladybird. What magnificent dogs they are too, as are the varied personalities of the dingoes.

The four pups have proven to be exceptional, and are being trained to do all sorts of tricks because they are so intelligent and have been socialised with people who come to visit. I got to meet all the dingoes, but when the pups came to greet me I was amazed at their friendliness, beautiful condition and intelligent behaviour. These four have the potential to really bring good publicity not only for the centre but for all dingoes. People love the look of them, and they are developing into real little show people. They know already how to put on an act. They are in good hands with Lyn and Peter, who have good experience in handling dogs of all sorts. Lyn and Peter are extremely careful to breed only those dingoes that have been DNA tested as pure bred to ensure the gene pool is kept strong. All of the dingoes are Alpine dingoes, except one that is a desert dingo.

'Dingo bitches usually come into season on Australia Day; they mate in March and have pups in May. That is the usual cycle. In Western Australia it happens a bit earlier. The amount of daylight on the retina of the eye seems to be the catalyst for the start of the cycle. In the desert country it is usually a bit earlier. We've proved over the years that any mating after the shortest day of the year – 22 June – means there will be no pups. I did an experiment here. The male dogs are usually infertile for the rest of the year when the bitches are not in season. However I had five litters in August and September, and proved that bitches can come back into season like cats – a silent cycle. It was very unusual to have pups in spring.'

In order to educate the public about the dingo, Lyn and Peter have taken their message to schools, shopping centres and festivals, as well as walking in main streets of towns. The Dingo Discovery Centre also has open days to introduce people to the group. 'The phone never stops,' says Lyn. 'We have fifteen people per session, and we have had over 500 people want to come and see the dingoes and the new pups. It was good for them to be super-socialised at an early age. The visitors will become good promoters for the centre and for the dingoes in general.'

While Lyn was off attending to her many dingoes, Peter and I wandered the home and he showed me all of his collection of dog-related memorabilia, and I wanted to learn more of how he became involved with it all.

'I was born in Melbourne in 1948, but spent a lot of time in the Cann River district in Gippsland, where my family owned farms. We were always off rabbiting as kids. Don't ever remember anyone talking about problems with dingoes back then, only rabbits and foxes. My first real meeting with dingoes was when I first met Bruce Jacobs at his dingo farm.

A Malaysian lady I knew wanted to see dingoes so I took her up to see them.

'I moved to Melbourne in 1960 to work and have spent all my working life in banking and finance, first with the ES&A Bank and then later on I became State Manager for AMP for a number of years, and between 2003 and 2005 I lived in India, where I went to set up a business for AMP. Now I own my own business doing financial planning.

'I was showing dogs in the 1970s and have always been keen on them. I've bred hundreds of golden retrievers over the years. I was top breeder three years in a row, which was a bit unusual, and I became the first elected president of KCC in 1992. I was president for four years. Lyn became vice president. I've been a dog judge for thirty years both here and overseas. We've judged every state of Australia as well as in Africa, India, the US, Canada, New Zealand, Malaysia, and in two weeks' time we are off to Peru to judge there, which has always been a goal of mine. I always had dogs when I was a kid; I had one that was best in the litter, so I showed it and won. I was hooked. It changed my life. I've won many shows over the years, including top two dogs in the Golden Retriever Club Speciality Show in 1998. Lyn and I met at a dog show. We've both been married before – I have two boys and a girl and two grandchildren, and Lyn has two boys from her first marriage. Our dogs are our kids between us.'

I asked how many dogs they had bred over the years. Lyn says, 'I've had hundreds of "best in show" dingoes and champions and have bred about 350 dogs. I'm recognised as a top breeder and top show judge; they are always wanting me to judge, but now we only judge overseas and don't show dogs any more. I have been judging for thirty-five years.'

Peter makes an interesting comment, which was echoed by Lyn. 'The pure bred dogs are doomed species. They now have such small gene pools, and we aren't really that keen on the way dog breeders and shows have gone.'

I mentioned, having seen some shows, that it appeared the contestants cared more about themselves, winning at all costs and the snobbery of it all, rather than the dogs themselves. Dogs at shows seemed bored or stressed. Whereas dogs in training or competing in events like sheep trials, fly ball or other fun sports seem happy and excited and love doing it. I know my own dog Dusty absolutely loves doing agility training, running flat out, weaving in and out of an obstacle course of hoops, tunnels, jumps, beams and poles. He loves socialising with other dogs at dog school and has fun. Dogs at shows, all preened and combed, pushed and prodded, never show any signs of excitement.

I asked Lyn how many dingoes they have had. 'Oh, I've bred well over 200 dingoes over twenty years, and we have many dingoes now all over Victoria, Western Australia, up as far as Broome and Karratha, and up to Bundaberg in Queensland, as well as all over New South Wales and some in South Australia. We supply to dingo fanciers and zoos and fauna parks.'

As I'd asked Peter some of his background, I did the same with Lyn.

'I was born in Murrumbeena, Melbourne in '42, and my brother and I always brought home any strays. We always had animals. I went to MacRobertson Girls School, and later went to work at the *Women's Weekly*, and then as a secretary in the ES&A Bank, then I went into the building industry. I saw my first dingo at Healesville Sanctuary as a kid, and I went back there on my own the day I got my driver's licence and sat by

the pen and watched. I knew then I wanted to have my own one day. I got my first dingo in 1988, a gift from Bruce Jacobs.

'I started to judge in 1969 and became an all-breeds judge. Peru will be the twentieth country I've judged in. I've had all sorts over the years; I had afghans (150 champions all up); I had a greyhound "dog of the year," and I also had italian greyhounds. I've been a student of dogs; I've studied anatomy and as a breeder I've researched. Many dog breeders chase the ribbons; they miss the big picture. I've learnt so many secrets from my dingoes I am reluctant to publish a book as I fear the dingo secrets may be used against the species by its enemies. My goal is to reintroduce the dingo back to the wild in a safe haven just for dingoes. Australian farmers have forever painted the dingo as the bogeyman of the bush. Our lives have been totally enriched by dingoes and dogs.

'Until you own a dingo you know nothing about dogs.'
See www.clix.to/dingodiscoverycentre/

Bat-makers

THE TINETTI FAMILY & JULIAN MILLICHAMP
CRICKET WILLOW: 'BIRTHPLACE OF THE AUSTRALIAN CRICKET BAT.'

Englishman Julian Millichamp was on holidays with his family in Australia. His eight-year-old son came out of a tourist information centre with a brochure he knew his dad would be interested in. Shortly after, when Julian walked up the long dirt driveway of Cricket Willow, he was caught by surprise when a man named Ian Tinetti said, 'You're Julian Millichamp, aren't you?' Ian knows a lot about cricket, and he knew he was talking to the man known as 'the prince of bat-makers', the man who made crickets bats for some of the best international test cricketers in the world.

Little did Ian Tinetti know what an impact that meeting would have on his business.

I decided to have a bit of a cricket month in January. I went to Cootamundra to see the cottage where Don Bradman was born, and the Cricket Captains' Walk for a look at the sculptures of Australian test captains, then on to Bowral to see the Bradman Museum as well. Then I came across the Cricket Willow brochure in a New South Wales tourist information centre, and a few days later I was browsing through a magazine and there was a story about the Tinetti family business. Seems I was meant to finish off January with cricket. It was the same brochure that led Julian Millichamp to the property.

If you want to know anything about Australia's greatest cricketer, you go to Bowral or Cootamundra. Melbourne's Cricket Ground is world famous. Sunbury, north of Melbourne, is the 'birthplace of the ashes', as any cricket lover knows. But if you want to know about how cricket bats are made then you should go to Tinetti's Hill at Shepherds Flat.

Where the hell is that? I hear you ask.

Well, it's north-west of both Melbourne and Sunbury. Get to Daylesford, spring-water and spa centre of Victoria, and you're close. Through Hepburn Springs, and just when you think you are lost, go up over Breakneck Gorge and just near Lavendula lavender farm you'll find it – Cricket Willow – 'birthplace of the Australian cricket bat' and home to the Tinetti family. And it's worth the effort to get there.

To trace how this 120-acre property became the home of the Australian cricket bat willow we go back to when the English cricket captain Archie MacLaren was talking to international test umpire Bob Crockett at the MCG test match on New Year's Day, 1902. During a break in play, MacLaren asked Crockett why there were no cricket willow trees growing in Australia. Consequently, when he returned to England MacLaren sent Crockett some cuttings. Six cuttings were sent from England, but only one survived the journey – barely. This single cutting was taken to Shepherds Flat in central Victoria where it was grafted by Bob Crockett's brother Jack, a horticulturist. Eventually, the Crockett Bat Company had 5000 trees growing along the river flats and the Crockett cricket bat became a household name amongst cricketers. Test cricketers Warwick Armstrong, Lindsay Hassett and Norman O'Neill all used Crockett bats.

Bob Crockett died in 1935 and his son J.R.M. continued the business. In 1956 R.M. Crockett & Son ceased business at Shepherds Flat. The business was sold to the Slazenger Group, and most of the trees were felled. When J.R.M. Crockett died his ashes were scattered across the site of the original plantation.

It was then that a dairy-farmer neighbour, Aquilino Tinetti junior (Ian's father), who had worked on the Crockett plantation, purchased the Crockett property and some of the cricket bat willow trees that were left along the Jim Crow Creek. Dairy cows replaced the willow groves. The few trees that remained were grown to keep the tradition alive in Australia.

In 1976 the dairy farm was sold on to Ian and Trish Tinetti. In 1987 the Tinetti family got a big shock when the milk contractor phoned to say that milk would no longer be collected from Shepherds Flat. It was the end of their dairy farm, and a new livelihood had to be found. It was when Melbourne cricket bat-maker Lachlan Fisher visited that a germ of an idea developed. Ian and Lachlan recreated the original willow plantations from cuttings of the trees that Ian's father had saved a quarter of a century earlier. The old chaff mill shed on the property was converted into a cricket-bat workshop. Lachlan set up his own business in Melbourne, while the Tinetti family turned their rocky front paddock into a flat picturesque cricket oval.

Hard work and determination meant that in 1999 the first cricket match was played on the oval. But work never stops at Cricket Willow.

When the Tinettis started to recreate the plantation there were only about ten trees left. Now 1000 trees make up the plantation, with another 4000 still in the nursery.

Ian and Trish Tinetti's children have a love of and great interest in the business. Adrian, twenty-six, is a lawyer; Nicole, twenty-five, is an accountant; Daniel, twenty-four, is an engineer; and Fiona, twenty-two, is a nurse. The whole family gets involved in activities and the cricket matches at Cricket Willow usually see more than one Tinetti take the field.

Ian is captain of the Cricket Willow team but says he is 'pretty well buggered now.' He was a good cricketer in his youth and played for Hepburn, Daylesford, South Melbourne, Caulfield, 'B' company in the army, Toowoomba in Queensland and Riverston in New South Wales. He started his first cricket scrapbook when he was four. His greatest thrill now is to see his kids play cricket.

Besides being the place to check out how cricket bats are made, Ian and Trish's small property is a 'field of dreams' – a cricket haven for others to enjoy. As well as their own cricket oval – complete with picket fence – they have numerous buildings such as the Cricket Gallery, which displays the process of making a cricket bat. Their Sam Morris Museum has displays with local history and tributes to sporting identities. Stumps Café is licensed and provides light meals and refreshments. The Hall of Sport has a full-size billiard table and on its walls there is a sporting memorabilia collection. Crockett Cottage is where workshops are held to show how finished cricket bats are oiled and boned. Backward Point is a bunkhouse and has a games

room for visitors. The Jabaroo Shop has cricket equipment for sale. Jabaroo is the Tinetti's own label. Cricketer's Cage is a fully enclosed training net complete with bowling machine. If you get sick of cricket, you can always go onto the bocce court or tennis court. Cricket Willow also offers its services for social and corporate cricket matches, school groups and cricket clinics, private functions and parties and guest speakers and tours.

And what happened to Julian Millichamp, the bloke who walked in one day for a look? Well, his life is a long history of cricket bat-making in itself.

Born in Staffordshire, England, Julian was taken on as an apprentice bat-maker in a small village in East Sussex. He learnt the trade from John Newberry, a master craftsman of Newberry & Co., who died in 1980. When Julian started his apprenticeship there was no electricity used: all bats were made totally by hand. His master was classed as one of the world's best bat-makers, and his ideas were ground breaking. When he joined Newberry, Julian was his first apprentice and just sixteen years old. Julian spent the next twenty-five years in the trade.

Julian later became founding partner of Millichamp & Hall in Somerset. International cricketers from across the globe sought out Julian's unique skill in tailor-making cricket bats. He became known as the world's premier bat-maker, supplying bats to a generation of sporting heroes.

By the late 1980s he was making bats for twenty-seven of the top forty-ranked batsmen in the world. He has made test bats for every continent. He says that now there are only a handful of pod shavers left in the world; all the rest of the bats are mass produced.

Julian says two outstanding people of the game he has made

bats for are Australian Adam Gilchrist – 'a gentleman of the game' – and West Indian Gordon Greenidge, who he describes as a 'super fella'. The worst in the game according to Julian was another West Indian who remains unnamed, but is described as 'full of himself'.

In 1981 Julian came to Australia but went on to set up a factory in New Zealand. For a hectic nine years he divided his time between summers in England and Australia and New Zealand, training apprentices and passing on the history of the trade along the way. With partner Jonathan Hall looking after their business in England, Julian joined forces with Puma Australia, and soon the Puma-Millichamp brand rose to prominence to become the bat of choice of test cricketers like Adam Gilchrist, Mark Taylor and Michael Bevan. In 1994 Julian sold his Australian business to Puma but continued to work for them until 2004.

After that, he decided it was time to seek new horizons and to see Australia with his family. So, with wife Tracey, daughters Madeleine, thirteen and Jocelynne, twelve; son Damon, ten; and a seven-year-old german shepherd/blue heeler cross called Rani, they packed their camper-trailer and spent the next six months travelling and camping. It was during that trip they ended up at a campsite at the base of Mt Franklin and had gone to Daylesford for a look when his son found the brochure for Cricket Willow. 'I was at the crossroads of my life, deciding what to do,' says Julian. 'It was September 2004, and we went back to Perth, packed up and moved here to Victoria in July 2005. We are living in Hepburn and we plan to buy a place, and so here we are.'

It was here in Victoria that Julian found the roots of Australian cricket bat-making – and a new challenge. He had decided he wanted to get back to the basics of the business and to create his own new brand – and so Screaming Cat was born.

'Screaming Cat has evolved from those early days of my career when, unlike today, all bats were individually graded on playability and performance. This unique art of grading through sound and feel, called "tapping up", is carried out with the simulation of a ball striking a bat by using a specially crafted mallet. I have fond memories of my mentor, whom upon tapping up the very best pieces of willow, would excitedly hail "It's a screaming cat, boy! A screaming cat!"'

Julian now uses the factory at Cricket Willow, where he makes Screaming Cat cricket bats. He is also making Jabaroo bats in conjunction with Ian. Both remain independent of the other but work closely together. Julian's cricket bat brand is sold through cricket specialists across Australia, continuing his very best efforts in handcrafting traditional cricket bats.

Ian comments, 'Here is the only place in the world where you can see the bat-making process from planting a willow tree through to use in the test arena.' One of the Tinetti mottos is 'bud to bat'.

Australia is lucky to have people still keen to preserve the tradition.

See also: www.screamingcat.com.au and www.cricketwillow. com.au

The Keeper of the Light

LEO OP DEN BROUW

'I WANTED TO BE AN ARCHAEOLOGIST OR A HISTORY TEACHER —
THE CLOSEST I GOT WAS DIGGING HOLES FOR PIPES.'

I wanted to interview Gabo Island's lighthouse keeper, but I found out he lived in Mallacoota. Some things are different nowadays. Leo Op den Brouw spends six weeks on Gabo and then another man takes over while Leo returns to his home in Mallacoota. Once, to work the light you had to live on site all the time. Since the federal government fobbed off lighthouses to state governments, things have changed. So, living in the far east of Victoria in a bush town and living and working on an island qualifies Leo as a bushie, I reckon.

Leo Op den Brouw has a long family association with boats and water. His great-grandparents were 'bargies' – people who worked and lived on the canals of Europe. 'They were basically the "truckies" of Europe; they would deliver all sorts of goods, like coal, potatoes, cement, and with all sorts of general cargo loaded they'd travel the rivers and canals of Holland, France, Belgium and Germany.' Even now his Auntie still lives on the family barge in Holland.

His father was born in Belgium and grew up on the family's 60-foot barge. 'The barge was commandeered by the Germans during the war. Dad joined the Dutch Merchant Navy, and later served in the navy, and then migrated to Australia. One day, when I win Tattslotto, I'd like to buy the family barge, ship it to Australia and put it on the water at Mallacoota,' he says with a smile.

Leo's home is filled with evidence of his passion for boats and the sea. The brass lamp from his grandfather's boat is on the wall, next to family photos, model boats he's built and an assortment of nautical items. A huge oil painting on the wall, done by his brother, is of his mother standing on the wharf next to the *Orion*, the ship they visited Holland on in 1963.

Leo grew up in the Dandenong Ranges, east of Melbourne, went to Kallista Primary School, then Monbulk High and finally Ferntree Gully Tech, where he completed a plumbing apprenticeship. His family always spent school holidays at Mallacoota, where Leo found his passion for the ocean. 'I started surfing at Torquay from about the age of seventeen and still love it.'

He was self-employed from the age of twenty-one in his trade, plumbing, and now at fifty-two, working the light is his job and passion. 'I have always been operating between Melbourne and Mallacoota. I took off overseas for three months surfing in Bali. I bought a block of land here in 1974; met my wife Kim in Mallacoota in 1978 and we married in 1979. I started building our home that same year. We moved here permanently and lived in a shed and a caravan during the three years it took to build the house. On my thirtieth birthday we moved into the house and we've been here ever since.

Leo and Kim have three daughters – Cassandra, twenty-six (married with three children); Thea, twenty-three (one child); and Bianca, nineteen (single, working and travelling in England and Europe).

I asked Leo's wife, Kim, now that all the children have left home, how does she handle having her husband away so much? 'For Leo, there was a honeymoon period, but then the reality of the isolation set in. Learning to be on my own took time. I have good friends, but it took some adjustment. There was a period of negativity, but we talked it through and made changes. We always talked through the process to cope. You have to have a willingness to change. We look out for each other, which has helped us to maintain a strong marriage. If you didn't have that, it wouldn't work. It's important to keep in touch with each other's feelings. I go out there occasionally during school holidays; we have an agreement with Parks Victoria to pay for me to make regular trips to the island, but visits are still infrequent.'

Kim is a primary school teacher, and she keeps busy with her commitments to the local prep to Year Twelve college, which has 143 kids. She has taught there for six years.

'I miss Leo heaps, of course. The first year was the hardest, with two of the three girls still at home. Now being on my own, my commitments keep me occupied. I have put my artistic pursuits on hold for a while; I love reading and doing crosswords and I have a strong network of friends, and I see them regularly. I also have a lot of preparation work at night to do for school. My church is also very supportive.

'Before taking up his position at Gabo, Leo was very

dissatisfied with his work – he needed a change. He is a multi-talented man, very passionate about the environment. I had serious concerns about how we'd cope, but I recognised that he needed a whole new direction. Once I decided it was right, I was happy for him; he's a real asset to Parks. He raised the bar level. He has a passion for history; he even has a little museum happening at the lighthouse with artifacts and information, and so on.'

Leo adds, 'I was a plumber from 1972 until 1999, and I still do a bit, but have scaled it right back. I was sick of the changes in regulations. Plumbing was okay, but I was also sick of being in overdraft and waiting to be paid. I always had the passion for boats, the sea, surf and history. Gabo is an icon.'

So how did he become a lighthouse keeper?

'I'm not. Actually, officially I am a "light station caretaker". A mate of mine had been on Gabo for about six years and I'd give him a hand, back as far as 1999, and then I got the job while he was away for a while. After the lights all went automatic, they were given back to the states. Previously they were in the hands of the Australian Maritime Safety Authority. Parks Victoria took over Gabo in 1992. The Kennett government wanted to sell them off.

'I started out on a short-term six-month contract, and I had two or three of those contracts. I thought it was a once in a lifetime opportunity – too good to miss. It was changed into a permanent shared position in 2001. I share the job with another bloke, the mate I started with. We started with a month on and a month off, but he's been away and so I'm doing six weeks on with two off.

'In the old days lighthouse keepers kept the light going and contractors did all the rest of the maintenance. Now it's the

opposite. Since the lights became fully automated, the contractors would do routine maintenance on batteries, lights, solar panels and that's all. They just come in now and then.

'Our job is very varied. We look after three houses, an airstrip, workshop, wind generator, remote power system, three diesel generators, tractor and implements, two diesel water-pumps, a jetty, a crane and large jetty shed (one of the oldest in Victoria). We maintain all that and mow the airstrip and the areas around the houses, make repairs to a 3-kilometre track, fencing, repair any housing problems, service the tractor. We also run the guesthouse accommodation, which sleeps eight and has a 70–80 per cent occupancy rate. We meet 'n' greet guests, drive them and their gear from the airstrip or the jetty. We conduct tours of the lighthouse, clean up when they leave, wash all the linen like a good housekeeper. We unload regular supplies of fuel and gas off the boat. We read weather observations for the Bureau of Meteorology four times a day. We also have small herds of cows to manage. Kikuyu grass is the worst, and I hate mowing all the time. Gabo is an amazing place with significant natural values in flora and fauna. The complex is 140 hectares. We have the largest little penguin colony with 30 000 pairs.

'Gabo Island is windy all the time from nor'-easterlies to howling sou'-westerlies. Salt spray is in the air all the time, which causes a lot of corrosion and rust. So we are always painting. Paint is guaranteed for seven years, but here we have to re-paint every two years. We have an old saying: "If it moves, grease it; if it doesn't then paint it." We have to paint in between the windy days.'

Leo's first impressions of Gabo Island? 'I had expectations of a windswept, isolated environment, with the only visible intrusion being Mallacoota. It has magnificent coastal scenery that is much the same as when Captain Cook went past. When tourists arrive they say, "What is there to do?" I say look at the wind direction and walk to the other side of the island. By the time they are ready to leave, they say, "We're coming back to see this and that next time." They always find a lot to do.

'Sometimes, when I get overloaded I go to the cemetery, which has been there since the 1860s, when the lighthouse was being constructed. It clears my head a bit and helps to put things in perspective; work is hectic at times. I went into the bush once to look for orchids and found a species not listed on the plant list (cinnamon bells). I work pretty hard, but I can find space to recharge. Sometimes in my free time I spend time making lighthouse sculptures out of old materials.

'I like to think my work is making a contribution to Gabo Island. I restored a timber panel in the lighthouse, and there behind the wall was numbering – and I thought, I am the first to see this since it was built all those years ago. I feel I'm part of the tradition to keep it all working for a purpose – to keep people safe when at sea. It's great to preserve an iconic piece of Australian history, and when I leave I'll know I've done a good job to make it happen. Over all the years I have been working towards that one purpose.'

Gabo is a special place. The sealers were here in about 1840, possibly earlier. There's a fair bit of Aboriginal history there too, groups from New South Wales and from Mallacoota met on Gabo; it's a pretty significant meeting place, although not much of it has been recorded. Initially only a temporary lighthouse was built here, but bureaucrats in Melbourne messed up and the keepers were left for months on end totally unaided.

Victoria doesn't realise that the island in one spot is just 500 metres from the mainland – depending on the sand gap. You wouldn't want to try and cross it, though, because it's a strong tidal area. The island is totally weather-dependent – both plane and boat need good weather to get in. Rough weather – then you are 'out there'.

'About twelve months ago we had continuous gales – fourteen days of blowing, no boat or plane in or out. I was completely isolated for fourteen days. That's when you have to be more careful with the axe. I'm then more deliberate in thought when undertaking tasks and thinking of potential hazards. After that sort of isolation, I bend the ears off a bit when I finally see people again.'

Do lighthouse keepers (light station caretakers) get lonely?

'I don't get lonely, but I miss some things. Chocolate éclairs. Apple turnovers with cream. I can't ration treats; I eat them all in two days. I do all my own pretty ordinary cooking, depending on how busy we are. We have a large freezer. We have fresh veggies from the garden. We supply all our own food, with monthly supplies.

'You can get burnt out. I had five months off and went to Western Australia then I was all raring to go again. I pace myself more now. I have some good projects to do, restoring an old table, restoring an old wooden sailing boat. Lighthouse people were historically all a little bit crazy: some drank too much and many became a bit "lightie" – went troppo or got cabin fever, call it what you want. Many spent too much time on their own.'

A talented man like Leo should have plenty to keep his mind occupied. I've seen some of his artistic work, his woodwork and more. He has always been a 'doer' – an Orbost shire councillor, and in numerous community groups like the State Emergency Service (twenty-five years), Coast Action Care Group, Surf Rider Club, and Ambulance Auxiliary.

'Kim is strong in her faith and wants to make a difference; we contribute to Compassion Australia, which sponsors children in developing countries, and Mercy Ministries, an organisation which provides safe houses for young girls in distress, and also Hands at Work in Africa, which teaches Africans to build sustainable houses and to become self-sufficient.'

And how does Leon sum his life and work up? He is a man who is content with his contributions.

'I wanted to be an archaeologist or a history teacher – the closest I got was digging holes for pipes,' Leo says with a laugh.

The Sculpture Garden

BRUNO TORFS

'I BELIEVE IN PLAY — LIFE IS TO BE ENJOYED.'

The township of Marysville is a small, beautiful village to the east of Melbourne and is the gateway to the mystic mountains region and the Yarra Valley, famous for its vineyards. It is a tourist haven and boasts all sorts of attractions. It has superb natural surrounds: fern gullies, mountain streams and Steavensons Falls, the highest waterfall in Victoria. Just off the main street you will find Bruno Torfs' Art & Sculpture Garden. You can't miss it, just look for the sculpture of the flying man out the front of the premises.

The first thing you notice when talking to Bruno Torfs is that he is pretty happy with his way of life. Bruno is not one to allow boundaries to restrict him. Ask him where he was born and he will simply reply 'South America' rather than tell you the country. He says he later moved to Europe, but again no specific country is mentioned. Ask him the size of his garden and he replies 'a few acres' even though he knows the measurements exactly. Boundaries, and the little boxes most people are categorised in, is not his way. He doesn't call himself a part of any country but considers himself to be a world citizen.

'I feel like I am not from anywhere in particular, I embrace all nations. I believe in play – life is to be enjoyed. I believe that we constantly create our own reality. I wake up in the morning and think, what can I do today?'

Bruno's life is very much in tune with nature and the beauty it brings to his life. In my job I usually ask many questions to do with dates, places and details, none of which is really Bruno. Although he allowed me to dig and delve and sometimes prod, I soon realised that this story would be different to some of the others, and that looking at his work would not mean that I'd get to know the full details.

I first visited Bruno's sculpture garden a few years ago and knew I'd be back to interview him. I love his work, his whimsical and poetic studies of people set in a tranquil bush garden leave people wanting more. I needed to know who this person was, this artist who created a garden so much in tune with his work. It is obvious that he has been a world traveller as this is very much reflected in his sculptures.

At the age of twelve Bruno's first oil painting was made using paint tubes his father had discarded, an old brush and a piece of scrap paper. Artistic talent runs in the family. 'My father Leonardo is eighty and still painting.' Leonardo Torfs is a renowned artist in Belgium. Bruno's artistic style was greatly influenced by the South American life he experienced as a youth.

'School and I didn't get on. It was not meant for me, and at fifteen I left school to begin as an apprentice sign writer and decorator, doing a lot of backdrops for movie billboards on the outside of buildings. I also attended the Academy of the Arts, which was situated opposite my workplace. I joined a night class for life drawing that was scheduled to run for six years although I finished the course in just fourteen months, almost five years ahead of schedule.

'A young sculptor named Staf Colruyt had a studio in the same building as my sign writing job. I spent lunch breaks looking at Staf's works and learning the practical techniques of the craft. I also met with Staf and other artists for sketching sessions where they would mostly sharpen their skills. I hadn't been interested in sculpture before I saw his work, but I soon saw the light and became very interested. I was twenty-three when I created my first sculpture.

'In my early twenties I had a brilliant plan to go back to the art academy to enrol in classical painting classes, not to study seriously, but to be near a beautiful girl, Marleen, who I had met two years earlier. Marleen and I married in 1979. In 1980 we both gave up our jobs and took off for France, Portugal and Spain. Shortly after, we embarked on a long trip through North and South America in a kombi van.' Together they were witness to great natural and cultural wonders, which Bruno loved to sketch.

On their return to Belgium, Marleen returned to full time employment while Bruno held annual exhibitions of his works from their home. Their first daughter Iris was born in 1982 and precisely two years later to the exact day, their second daughter Klaartje was born.

Bruno's work has been inspired by the many lands he has travelled in. He has explored India, Nepal, Bali, Peru, Ecuador,

Java, Turkey and Spain. He has travelled to twenty-four countries and intends to visit many more. Bruno was particularly inspired by his experiences in India and Ecuador. It was the exciting and adventurous life that would see him sketch in the field of a foreign land and then return home to create sculptures and paintings. This way of life continued for twelve years. Bruno embarked on many adventures such as crossing the vast deserts of Rajasthan on camel back, a perilous train journey into the Andes, trekking through the Himalayas on foot and traversing India on a bicycle. He *really* saw the countries he was visiting, not as a tourist quickly hopping from one hotel to another.

At the age of fourteen he wrote in his diary that one day he wanted to live in Australia. He arrived when he was forty – some ten years ago. He had a sister living in Victoria's Mornington Peninsula. 'We wondered what she was doing in Australia, and so we visited her and everything said to me that "Australia's waiting." It is hard to get permission, but we just went with the flow and we eventually ended up here. I was keen to create a sculpture garden and make everything more attractive. Plants are as important to the garden as the sculptures.'

Marleen is an artist too, and she is mainly interested in silk painting. Iris is a young mother and also interested in music and art. Klaartje is a florist and paints. Bruno says, 'For me, vision is important. For me, the real art is to live our lives without any friction; any limitation is pain. The mind creates limitations all the time. There is adventure in seeing who we really are, how fresh we can be by not falling back into routine.'

I asked Bruno how many people visit the sculpture garden every year, and as I should have expected, instead of exact figures he just casually says 'thousands'. The attendance figures grow each year as word spreads, and no doubt word of mouth is always positive when talking about his garden because it is an amazing collection.

I wanted to know what the sculpture garden was like when he started.

'We started in February 1996 and opened to the public in August of the same year. We worked hard. Many areas were covered in blackberries and bracken which we removed by hand. Meanwhile I created sculptures. It was a very busy, productive and exciting time. Now there are over three hundred works on display. About one hundred and thirty sculptures reside in the garden; the other works, being either paintings or sculptures, are exhibited in the gallery.'

None of Bruno's works are for sale. They are part of his life and he is happy to share them with everyone. He is not really interested in doing commissioned works either, although he did show me a sketch of a piece he agreed to create for the shire. He believes that his quality of life is more important than the pursuit of money.

I asked him how long it takes him to make a life-size sculpture of a person, like many of those in his garden.

'This is probably the number one question I get asked by people who visit the garden. Mostly, I have a fixed picture in my mind of what I want to create before I start, and then on average, one sculpture takes about a week to complete.'

When you look closely at the detail in Bruno's work you see many little hidden things. One humorous thing that most people miss is a sculpture of the man who has mice all over him. Bruno has used mice to create the statue's facial features and most people don't even notice. There are, in fact, over twenty mice on that sculpture alone. Also, many people never look up;

if they did, they would see, sitting in a tree, a sculpture in a large bird's nest built by Bruno. These are a couple of secrets that I have discovered, the rest you will have to find yourselves. There are many whimsical attributes to the sculptures as well as the peaceful, the cultural and the comforting. Words cannot adequately convey what the sculpture garden is really like – you just simply have to visit it yourself; you will not be disappointed.

Bruno's sculpture garden is on Falls Road, Marysville – just follow the big signs on the main street. It truly is a paradise for art and garden lovers. I highly recommend it to all. And while you are there make sure you get a copy of Bruno's lavish book of photographs of some of his works.

And so finally it was time for me to leave, but I wanted to know where it all goes from here. Bruno said that now 'is the time to fine-tune the garden. A little four-year-old girl who was visiting with her family suggested that we should have a unicorn in our garden. Would you believe, that same day I saw a white horse in the nearby paddock – what energy, good luck and beauty. So yes, I have started working on a unicorn for the garden.'

I now have a suggestion for a sculpture too, but I'll save it for the next time I see Bruno and his magical garden. I have also started making sculptures myself, thanks to the inspirational Bruno Torfs.

Jimmy Possum

MARGOT & ALAN SPALDING

'IF WE COULD HAVE MADE $70 000 A YEAR, WE'D HAVE BEEN HAPPY.'
JIMMY POSSUM'S TURNOVER LAST YEAR WAS
IN EXCESS OF $13.2 MILLION.

'You must be Jimmy Possum's wife, then?'

As co-owner of Jimmy Possum Furniture, Margot Spalding has heard that one before. She can blame her husband Alan for the unusual name of their business. They were looking for a name that was both whimsical and memorable. Alan had been reading a book about 'Possum', a recluse who lived in the bush along the Murray River. Alan liked the sound of him, and he'd also heard stories about a man named Jimmy Possum, a furniture maker who lived in the north-west of Tasmania in the late nineteenth century; he supposedly lived in a tree. His work was regarded as excellent, and today a single chair of his brings as much as $1500 at auction. Not much else is known of him, but Alan thought it was a good name. Margot wasn't sure about the name, but after saying it for a while grew to like it, and so that's how the Jimmy Possum Furniture empire came into being.

Why did a couple with seven kids decide to start a furniture company?

Both Alan and Margot had worked as teachers in the past. Alan was a furniture maker. Margot was also manufacturing kids' clothes. Later on, because of Alan's skills as a furniture maker, they operated the California Gully Traditional Furniture Company in outer Bendigo. The recession put an end to that business, and so it was time for a change. They built a corrugated iron house on some land at Harcourt and 'Alan went through his farming stage,' as Margot puts it. He tried almost everything – raspberries, chestnuts, yabbies, emu, deer, grapes and more. Margot was working in a furniture store and learnt a lot from her friend, the owner. They attended furniture shows across Australia and saw what the industry was like and what people wanted.

'One night in 1995 Alan and I sat down and discussed what we could do to earn some dollars, and finally we decided we'd become a wholesale manufacturer and supply stores.' Margot remembers how their business got going at home in a shed. 'I remember saying to Alan when we borrowed $15 000 to buy a panel saw and a kit shed that we didn't need such a big shed. It was about 60 feet by 30 feet. We had one employee. We sold only to two stores: one in Bendigo and one in Melbourne.

'Six months later we took a range of furniture to show and I sold nine months' worth of work that had to be delivered in ten weeks. Alan thought I was crazy and that we'd never do it. We delivered in twelve weeks and only lost one store because we didn't deliver on time. He later regretted cancelling on us, though.'

Margot went on the road full time, selling to stores. They moved into a leased building – an old soft-drink factory – and employed another two people to meet demands.

In 1996 and '97 six people were employed and Jimmy Possum furniture was being sold in six stores. By 1998 there were seven people and a part-time cleaner. The following year fourteen people were employed, including the part-time cleaner and one apprentice; by this time Jimmy Possum were supplying thirty stores Australia wide.

It was time to move to a larger property. And by 2000 the workforce had grown to thirty-three people, including the part-time cleaner, a truck driver, a company representative and five more apprentices, and they were now supplying some forty-three stores. A 10-tonne truck was purchased for deliveries.

They built a new factory in front of the old one, then another behind it, and then another one beside it. Their property is now full. The next move in a few years time will have to be to totally new premises elsewhere.

By 2001 employees totalled forty-two, including nine apprentices, three of whom were female, and they supplied over fifty stores. In 2002 Jimmy Possum opened their first store in Brisbane, and in 2003 the Jimmy Possum Designer Showroom opened in Collingwood, Melbourne, followed by another in 2004 in Fitzroy, Melbourne. Following close behind the Melbourne showrooms, they opened their first store in Sydney at Waterloo. In 2006 they opened stores in Cheltenham in Melbourne, and in Mosman in Sydney. 'The Mosman store had to be doubled in size after just three months,' says Margot. 'Many people had said we couldn't do this in fashionable North Shore Sydney, but we took part of Bendigo to Sydney; we didn't change to be part of Sydney, and they love it.'

From only working on a limited range, Jimmy Possum now makes a wide range of furniture, including dining, occasional, entertainment, bedroom, home office and sofas in ten different styles, ranging from country to contemporary – all up, in excess of 1000 items. Both new and recycled timber is used. Cushions are also made, and they even produce original artworks.

Jimmy Possum employs 100 people at the factory and another fifty in stores. As well as the 10-tonne truck, there is a 20-tonne truck now and a large Jimmy Possum delivery van – and a four-wheel drive ute for sourcing timbers and delivering as far away as Brisbane.

'One of the reasons for the success of the business is how we operate,' says Margot. 'We only supplied to selected stores, not the big national stores, but to independent operators who have a passion for their business and who take a whole range of our products, not just a few items. We supplied to only one store in town, never have more than one store in an area with our products. They got the exclusive rights to our products, and we are very particular in who we choose. We saw the big retailers moving towards Chinese-made imports purely for the profit, where we are keen to supply good Australian-made products and be at the top end of the market. We are committed to values; we live those values and believe if you are friendly and loyal, you will succeed.'

Alan adds, 'We were originally happy to aim for a good wage and to employ six to eight people. We still have trouble comprehending just how successful it's been. We are still living the dream, and I never want to retire.'

The business has been built for the future. As Margot says, 'We have so many children and now grandchildren, too. Many have shown an interest in working in the business;

we wanted to have a business large enough to accommodate their individual and varied skills and interests, without them conflicting or competing with each other. For instance, of the seven children, five work in the business. Jessica spends three days a week painting original artworks at our home studio for our stores; Emily is a creative writer who is a retail trainer and works in marketing and PR; Georgia is an industrial designer and manages marketing and merchandising; Eliza manages the two Melbourne stores; Todd is at the factory coordinating design and development. All the design work is done by Todd, Alan and me.'

The training of good staff has always been important. One apprentice won Best Apprentice for every year of his training at college. One year, five Jimmy Possum apprentices won every year level 'apprentice of the year' awards at Bendigo TAFE. There are now thirty-five young apprentices working at Jimmy Possum. 'It's great to give kids a chance,' says Alan. 'In the early days we couldn't afford to employ tradesmen and had long-term unemployed people, but these young apprentices are the future and it is good for Bendigo.'

Jimmy Possum gives awards for woodwork to six local schools each year. It also has fourteen work-experience students a year to give students some ideas about their future career.

As Alan and I walk from one end of the factory to the other, he shows me all the various processes and what the staff do. As a timber lover, I was keen to know more about what they use. 'We use 50/50 new and recycled timber. We have three suppliers of new timber. Good second-hand material is easier to find than good new timber. We use Victorian Ash sourced locally from Melbourne. Most of it comes from Melbourne from old flooring and stud frames: it is much better than new timber. We have seven different timber stains, five of which are used on recycled works.' He is pleased to add, 'We are the biggest user of recycled timber in Australia.'

'Jimmy Possum has been good for Bendigo,' says Margot. 'We love the life here. Our factory looks out across paddocks near a forest full of kangaroos. Bendigo has been a wonderful place to rear lots of kids and we are proud to support many Bendigo families, suppliers and organisations.'

Margot is the driving force behind the selling of Jimmy Possum furniture. She was named Telstra Australian Businesswoman of the Year for 2006. The business has been hard at times, she says, and she has shed many tears and survived many years on very little sleep, but she is also a focused and driven woman. She believed she could juggle a large family with a growing business and proved it.

Alan also spends a lot of time focusing on the future of the business. 'Jimmy Possum is still a dream come true. When we started if we could have made $70 000 a year, we'd have been happy. Our turnover in the first year was $60 000.'

He doesn't add that their turnover last year, just eleven years later, was in excess of $13.2 million and in 2006–07 will be in excess of $20 million.

I wonder what the real Jimmy Possum would think if he walked into the factory today?

Dog Trapper

MARG KRELLE

'I'VE HEARD THEM MANY TIMES, BUT IT STILL GIVES ME
A COLD SHIVER EACH TIME.'

Margaret Krelle is the only registered female dog trapper in Victoria. One of the late Ron Krelle's proudest moments was when he had his photo taken with his son and daughter while they were duck shooting. Not many fathers could say they went duck shooting with both their son and daughter. Margaret Krelle has been shooting for as long as she can remember. The moment I saw her being interviewed on ABC-TV I knew I had to meet her. She is a bushie through and through.

Marg says that she hates the job of trapping and shooting wild dogs, but it's necessary work and she's proud to be doing a good job. She has seen the terrible damage that wild dogs can do to sheep flocks and their lambs. In August 2006 farms to the west of her territory lost 332 sheep in less than a month.

'In the north-west of Victoria we have four registered dog trappers – southern is Terry Miller and myself, and northern is Bob Brown and Kevin Heintzke. We are funded by the Good Neighbour Program.

'Many people just don't understand why we trap and shoot them, but if they saw what we see, they would. I love dogs and have three of my own that I adore, and they are so much a part of my life. Wild dogs, however, are a terrible menace. One wild bitch will teach her pups how to kill, ripping the bellies from sheep and leaving them to die in agony. I've seen sheep chased into the bush where, in their desperate attempts to escape, they have become impaled on sharp sticks and branches and are unable to get off and escape. They are then attacked by dogs and with their stomachs hanging on the ground are left to die a terrible death.'

The minute you meet Marg, you sense she is a friendly bushie – self reliant and capable. She is a woman of the land. She lives on the farm her grandparents started and her home is the one her grandparents built in 1912; it has been nicely restored and very much has the feminine touch. 'It's home,' says Marg – home to her and her great little Jack Russell dog called Ruger, named after a .22 rifle.

Her mother Edna (known by everyone as Susie) lives in a house next door that she and Ron built when they were first married. The Krelle family farm is 2500 acres. It is now share-farmed on one block and leased on the other two blocks. Some 1900 acres is sown down with wheat, barley, lupins and peas. Marg still has thirty-five murray greys – her father always had cattle.

'I went to Melbourne in 1981 to study to become a hair-dresser. I later worked in a salon at Donald three days a week, but then I was asked to go back to Melbourne to teach hair-dressing, which I did for about four years until 1990.'

The bush was in her blood, and eventually home called again. She returned to help on the family farm as her brother Leon left to follow his football dream in Adelaide. He is now married with two kids and lives in Horsham, where he works for a chemical company.

'We'd always trapped rabbits as kids, but I remember when I was about eight or nine I saw my first wild dog that had killed sheep. When I was about sixteen we were looking after Uncle Jim's farm while he was away and one wild dog – a bitch – killed eighty-six sheep in two nights. So I first started trapping with Dad, who taught me a lot.

'He died in 2001, the year we finally got some real help for a control program of wild dogs with the government. Dad always had staghounds and trapped wild dogs all his life, and his father, my poppy, did too. Since 1997 I've kept really good trapping records and I can't believe the number of dogs. The numbers aren't decreasing, but the sheep numbers aren't as high, many farms don't have sheep at all now. Just as well, or we'd have many more deaths due to dog attacks.

'I was put in the deep end and had to learn – Dad always called me "the apprentice". Dad was still learning about dogs, too, and he'd been doing it all his life. I'm always learning; every dog is different – they are very smart. Sometimes in February or March they will walk right past the traps; often it takes a lot of work to catch one dog. Sometimes it takes rain to wash away all smells to help the trap site to be fresh.'

Marg and I left the family farm near Lake Albacutya, north of Rainbow, and headed bush in her four-wheel drive to go check on a line of traps she had set. Legally, she is required to check her traps every two days. Times are different now. Her father didn't get his first dog traps until the late 1970s; before then they just used rabbit traps. Steel-jaw traps were replaced with rubber-jaw traps in 2001. Until that time they were not allowed to trap on public land. 'Now we trap in the park, but we have warning signs up and we work in consultation with Parks staff.'

We drove to an area known as Booligal, farm land next to the Wyperfeld National Park in Victoria's north-west mallee country. As we drove along the boundary fences, on one side of the ute was cropped farming land and the other side was thick mallee bushland – home of the wild dogs. It was a hot day with very strong winds and dust was in the air. A lousy day to be in the open.

Every so often Marg would stop the vehicle to check where she had laid a trap. For the uninitiated there was nothing to see, the large steel trap was hidden beneath sand. She had bright pink tape tied on a tree or fence nearby and a sign stating the danger of 'dog trapping implement' nearby.

All the traps we visited were empty. Through the sandy tracks we headed toward the China Wall – a long line of sand dune covered bush. Everywhere we travelled was sandy four-wheel drive country, dirt tracks that would bog any other vehicle.

Marg is easy company to be with; she is a nice lady to share a yarn and a laugh with. She has many stories to tell. While we were checking on the traps, she was keeping an eye on the skies and an ear on the radio. There was a fire to the north of us. The northern skies were smoke filled – a so-called control burn by the Department of Sustainability and Environment (sometimes jokingly called the Department of Sparks and Ash) had escaped, and the radio said it had already swept through 8000 acres and was still burning (by the next day it had burnt over 20000 acres). Marg is a member of the local fire brigade and was listening keenly to reports of the fire's progress, expecting a call out later that day. We returned our conversation to wild dogs.

'The dog-trapping season can vary greatly, depending on the weather, rain particularly. In a normal year I trap from October through to May, and on average get thirty-eight dogs a year. In 1997 I got ten wild dogs in fourteen days – all the same size and age, both black-and-white and black-and-tan. However in 2002–03, around Lake Albacutya, Archibold Track, Nine Mile Square, I trapped sixteen dogs in ten days. Never seen so many before. In a bad year I might trap only from November to January.

'In summer when the water dries up out in the scrub the dogs come out of the bush. There're less sheep now, so the mobs get a hammering from dogs, they usually hang around a while before attacking sheep. They don't know what the sheep are because they are used to killing native animals like emus and kangaroos. If a sheep is being mauled this usually means young dogs, because they don't know how to kill yet. Old dogs just come in and kill outright. It's always good to see which way a dog comes into a paddock, not just at water sites. You could put a trap down near water (like a dam), but it may be entering a paddock from a totally different direction.'

You soon gather when talking with Marg that she has broad knowledge not only about her job but also of the bush. She says much of the knowledge is disappearing; the old blokes have died. Ever since her own father died she has had good help from Terry Miller, another trapper at Yanac. He was taught by his father many years ago.

'Terry is good; he taught me how not to catch pigeons, hares or rabbits in traps – just dogs. There are a lot of secrets. Terry works from the netting fence to Pine Plains. He's a great trapper.

'In 2001 the government finally started funding a program and now we get reimbursed the cost of diesel fuel and also our time. We have to keep good records and submit time sheets to the Department of Sustainability and Environment. I keep photos and detailed information of everything I do. This book is my bible. Every trap I own is numbered. I'm also accredited to shoot in National Parks as well.'

A round trip of Marg's territory could be 212 kilometres or even more. 'The main rule I have is to never go into the bush alone. My father had the same rule. Let me say, if I got caught in a dog trap in the bush, I don't want to be alone. One in ten dogs will drag a trap and some can do it for miles. To find a dog means you have to be a long way from your ute. No one would find you in this country if you were alone and trapped.'

Marg now has help from Andrew Shilling from Rainbow. His family owns an adjoining property, and he also was taught by Ron Krelle how to trap dogs. He is now Margaret's 'apprentice'. Although on this day there were no dogs in the traps, I did get to see the results of Marg's trapping work. The 'dog tree' had ten dead dogs hanging from a steel bar between two trees.

Marg set a trap for me to photograph, but she keeps some of her secrets to herself and only showed me part of her 'system'. She doesn't want inexperienced people trying to do the same, and fair enough, too. 'I've had a few people trying to get information, but why should we give out information to amateurs?' She has also had some abuse because of her job from people who simply do not understand why it's done. I wanted to know what sort of dogs she gets in her traps. Were they just dogs escaped from towns or farms or were they wild dogs born and bred in the bush over many generations?

'These are real wild dogs. Most dogs we get are black-and-tan but occasionally we get a yellow dog. The nearest breed they look like is kelpie, but the wild dog is very distinctive – short tail, heavy-set front, boof-head, pricked ears. They don't know what fences are; they can't jump a fence and will always look for holes to get through. We don't see them much, only an occasional short glimpse of them – they are wild and will avoid you at all costs. In a trap a dog will always want to get away. They'll be frightened of you and won't challenge you or show their teeth, normally. They always try to avoid you. They particularly hate motorbikes, and when tourists are about you don't see or get dogs. The wild dogs are smaller than domestic dogs, although in the last few years there have been some really big ones (17–19 kilos), mainly males. Females are usually smaller in size. The other distinctive thing about wild dogs is that their front paws are bigger than the back ones. They are born with short tails, and even small pups I've taken have got little tails. They do not yelp or bark, and their eyes are green in colour.

'In the early years, dogs were mainly black in colour, but now we get tans, greys, black-and-yellows. Terry Miller hardly ever gets tans or yellows. Just seems to be different dogs in different areas. Dad always said they were the true native wild dog, like the dingo, because of their distinctive features.

'I feel the bigger dogs have come from another area, probably South Australia, where there has been plenty of food and water. Most of our dogs are small and in poor condition. In my

territory wild dogs are found from the netting fence around the edge of the Crown land, Wyperfeld National Park, Booligal, Lake Albacutya, up to the Wyperfeld entrance, not around the Pine Plains.

'I get to see pups here, but Terry Miller hasn't seen many, and neither have the blokes in the northern section. I'd like to know where they have their pups. Dad and I went out to the Granites, thinking that it would be a good spot for them with caves there, but no sign. We camped on a track as we had a flat tyre, and in the morning it was a white frost and tracks showed that two dogs had come within 50 metres of our camp, but turned around to avoid us.

'I grew up with all the old dog trappers like my dad, uncles, and other blokes like Fred Saul senior, and they all had wild dog stories. I remember asking Pop once about a sore on one of Fred's dogs. He said a wild dog had bitten it and the wound healed but then kept coming back again and again. If a sheep survives a wild dog attack, they will never be any good again. Dad always said, give it five days, if it's still alive, it will be tame (domestic) dogs gone wild that attacked, but if it gets worse or dies, it will have been a wild dog attack. Wild dogs usually attack the back legs and the flanks of sheep. Tame dogs usually attack the neck and bellies and usually only eat the heart and lungs, etc. if they are hungry.'

Marg's knowledge of dogs has come from spending all her life learning about them. She has seen just how smart the wild dogs really are. 'We have seen dogs that just know where the traps are and would jump the trap, so we'd put a second one behind it, but it would jump both traps. Dad once had four traps lying in a line in a gateway, and still the dog jumped all four. We ended up getting that dog by laying a trap back down the track as well. He had used the track hundreds of times when he was coming into the bore and knew where it was safe. He was a big black-and-white dog and the only one that bared teeth at me. It was because I was standing in the way of his freedom. Dad was behind the dog and I had run in a half circle through the bush to get in front of him.

'Dad kept yelling out and asking if I could see the dog, and I yelled "Yes." He said, "Well, shoot the bloody thing," but I couldn't because Dad was in the line of fire, so he hid. He was behind the small mallee tree but he was a big man. When I shot the dog he yelled out, "Did you get it?" I said yes, and he said, "Thank God for that," but he was rubbing his legs from the shotgun pellets. We laughed about it in the ute on the way home. Uncle Jim Saul could also see the funny side of that story. Him and Dad were best mates and Jim would always call in for a cuppa, or Dad and I always called into his place 'Booligal' when we went bush. At the Bore Block on Booligal is a good place to listen to the wild dogs howl. Nothing like a domestic dog bark, but a real howl. I've heard them many times, but it still gives me a cold shiver each time.'

I had many questions about wild dogs and Marg didn't hesitate to share her thoughts. I must say I felt very much in awe of her: she has that understated but in-depth knowledge of the bush. In the old days they referred to people with that knowledge as being a 'real bushman'. Marg would have fitted in quite well with any of them.

'Wild dogs seem to travel the same path a lot. I think it's because of watering points, soaks, dams and bores. Water has a big part in it; they follow old tracks that back in the 1890s and 1920s the old settlers on horseback would have followed.

'A while ago I saw a dog watching me as I drove past the

China Wall. A couple of weeks ago I sat and watched a black dog that was watching me from on top of a rise. Once he smelt me, he was off over the ridge but I had watched him for ten minutes. Usually you don't get to see them much at all. They seem to not know what a human is other than they know to avoid you. Over a period of time they will get used to you camping in the bush and get closer each day and end up going through your camp. They sit in the bush and just watch you. Even when caught in a trap they won't move until you get out of the ute and go towards them.'

Some weeks after I spent time with her, Marg told me she got a new sensor trap with a data computer on it to monitor movement in front of the trap and to relay a signal when the trap goes off. 'I'm not having much luck with it at the moment,' she says. 'Too many smells and things; dogs notice any changes like that.'

Back at the family farm it's time for a cuppa and a yarn with Marg's mum Mrs Krelle, and a play with little Ruger and a pat for the two old farm dogs, the friendly Nugget and Socks. Their days of work are over and they get to enjoy some well-earned peace at home. Ruger chews on a stick underneath the kitchen table as Mrs Krelle and Marg show me photos of Ron Krelle and his days of shooting, fishing and farming. Marg also shows me a dog pelt that her father got when he was just sixteen years old, a yellow dog that he trapped.

This is a typical Aussie bush family and the songs that were sung at Ron Krelle's funeral are typical of the bushies – 'She's My Ute', 'Cunnamulla Fella' and 'Leave Him in the Longyard'. The family motto is 'family endures forever'. Ron Krelle can rest in peace knowing he did his job well and taught his mates well. His 'apprentice' is well trained and doing a terrific job.

Typical of bush Aussie hospitality, Mrs Krelle doesn't let me leave without taking two dozen eggs from her free-range chickens. I leave knowing I have a better understanding of Marg's job – it's not a pleasant job, but one that people of the bush understand as part of the life on the land.

Real Treasure

RACHAEL TREASURE

'I ARRIVED IN A UTE AND MY THREE BRIDESMAIDS WERE
ACCOMPANIED DOWN THE AISLE BY MY DOGS.'

To get to Rachael's place you turn off near Black Charlie's
Opening but before Bust-Me-Gall Hill, in the central-eastern
bush country of Tasmania. Follow the dirt track a few miles,
and when you get to the place with all the dogs, just yell out,
'Stick the billy on, Rachael.'

There's a fair chance she will know you are coming by the
barking of her dogs, or else she will see you coming anyway
from her office window, where she'll be working on her next
bestselling book. Rachael Treasure is a bushie born and bred.

'Rattie', as she is known to her friends, was born in Hobart in
1968 and is married to another bushie – John, from the Dargo
High Plains in Victoria, who is one of the famous Treasure
family, and comes from a long line of cattlemen.

Her kelpies, her writing and her two young children are all

huge parts of Rachael's life. I followed the dusty track to see Rachael, and we had an afternoon of yarning, cuppas – and dogs!

Rachael Treasure is the bestselling author of *Jillaroo*, *The Stockmen* and *The Rouseabout* – books that have won the hearts of readers, particularly bushies; novels about the Australian country and its way of life.

We had been corresponding by email and it was obvious we shared a huge passion for dogs. To meet her in the flesh and spend time with her as well as her dogs was a joy. This is one talented lady.

When we first met she was nearing the birth of her first child, but now she has a girl and a boy – Rosie and Charlie. We've kept in touch on the phone and through emails and we will meet again this year.

Rachael and John are in farm partnership with her father, Val, and run 2000 merino sheep on 3000 acres of both leased and private country. They've also just gone back into running poll herefords and breeding waler stockhorses to continue John's childhood connection with cattle and working horses.

'It was my aunt Susie who interested me in shearing and got me onto horses. As a child I was obsessed with animals. I used to impersonate English dog expert Barbara Woodhouse for a joke by putting on my granny's tweed skirts, but Barbara turned out to be an inspiration. It was my mum who nurtured my interest in literature and art. But with a strong farming background it was evident to me I would one day write a book about the bush and have as many working dogs as possible.

'I was always going to be a writer, especially one with a strong rural perspective. A writer's tip I heard was "write about what you know". Farming, rural people, dogs and the natural environment are my passions, so of course form the basis for many of my works. I remember Mum saying to me, "You can't write about life until you experience it fully." So I chose to jump into life boots and all.'

Rachael loved the bush life. And it would seem her love of dogs stems back to her grandfathers, Ron Smith, farm labourer and rabbiter, who had thirty-seven rabbit dogs, and Archie Wise, who had a reputation for being a wonderful, gentle stockman.

While Rachael was always comfortable with 'shovelling sheep manure', she knew becoming a journalist would give her employment as well as discipline.

'The whole reason for me leaning towards journalism was so I could eventually do fiction. I had won a few awards for short story writing, and with the assistance of the Tasmanian Writers Centre I received a mentorship. I've been on the Tasmanian Writers Centre Board, too.' She laughs and says, 'But, I think I'm more used to the shearing board and that's where I intend to stay.'

After a year working in sheds in western New South Wales, Rachael then went to Orange Agricultural College. She later went on to study print journalism and gained a BA (Communication) from Charles Sturt University in Bathurst. Her journalistic career kept her very much in touch with the rural community. After a year reporting on a Tasmanian newspaper, she spent a year on ABC rural radio, then two years as a dairy writer for *Stock & Land*, followed by freelance work for *Weekly Times* and *Outback*. Her first script for television, *Albert's Chook Tractor*, was made into a drama for SBS-TV.

In between jobs, Rachael managed to fit in backpacking around twenty countries across the world.

Rachael met her husband-to-be, John, at Ringers nightclub

in Sale, Victoria. 'It was his RM Williams boots that caught my eye,' she says. John is a fifth-generation high country cattleman from near Stratford in Victoria, and together they helped run trail rides and droving trips into the Dargo High Plains.

'Our wedding was a real bush affair – more like a cattleman's get together. We were married at our property beside a river and under a gum tree. I arrived in a ute and my three bridesmaids were accompanied down the aisle by my dogs. John rode a horse to the altar.'

Rachael and John still fly back and forth from Tasmania to Victoria to work with John's family. John is now working two days a week as a teacher at a tiny bush school that has only twenty-two children. But both John and Rachael have been teaching people outside the classroom and in the sheep yards.

'I wanted to learn the art of dog training, so in 1997 I took my dog Dougall to a two-day working dog education school at Paul McPhail's property in Welshpool, Victoria. It was a course that changed my life, and made me realise the power of communicating effectively with animals.'

Rachael was so obsessed with her dog that she did a few courses with Paul until he asked her to assist him. She agreed, and they have since held demonstrations at Tasmania's AgFest Agricultural Show followed by Working Dog Schools. She and John have now formed the Tasmanian Kelpie & Collie Collective, which is hosted at her website and is basically a bunch of mates who help farmers find good working dogs and trainers across the nation.

In 1998 John and Rachael decided to go to Queensland to work on a cattle station, and ended up on Rolleston, south of Emerald, 'but near nowhere'. While John worked cattle full time, Rachael worked as a jillaroo part time and wrote part

time. Her work saw her doing everything from cattle mustering to cleaning toilets. It was like a dream come true, especially when she did camp cooking. 'Work was cattle, ringers, helicopters and motorbikes.'

By late 2000 *Jillaroo* was finished, and after a lengthy period of editing and getting it to print, her dream was realised in 2002 – her first novel, *Jillaroo*, became a bestseller.

Jillaroo is about a young Aussie woman who throws her swag in the ute and heads north to work as a jillaroo. It is as Aussie as blue singlets and Blundstone boots. There is a big part of Rachael in her writing. She writes with passion. She admits that the women in her books are partly based on herself and her friends in the bush.

'For me it was a dream fulfilled. It is also a starting point. It is a voice for the young rural community. It's great to have a novel out there to inspire. I wrote it for young rural people.

The book is about life in the bush, B&S balls and more.'

All Rachael really wanted from the money she hoped to earn from book sales was enough to buy materials to build flash dog yards and buy a second-hand twin-cab ute. Well, let me tell you she got the ute – and the dog yards.

When she returned to Tasmania after finishing writing the book in Queensland, Rachael noticed an ad in the paper calling for a person to train as a sniffer-dog handler. She applied and got the job – two days a week for three months. This was dog-handling with a difference. She was supplied with a dog, a springer spaniel called Tiny, and together they work each season in the truffleries of Tasmania.

The truffle industry only started in Tasmania in 1995 and is still a closely guarded business. Truffles are a sort of underground mushroom, a rare delicacy and worth more than gold. In France they bring many thousands of dollars each. Rachael loves the work because it's outside, with dogs and other great country girls.

The success of her first novel meant she was soon in demand as a guest speaker, doing book signings and radio interviews. She was already working on another novel when we first met.

The year 2002 brought another sort of success for Rachael. One of her dogs, ten-month old Taxi, from her kelpie stud breeding program, was presented at the famous Casterton Working Dog Auction in Victoria. It was the first time Tasmanian dogs were offered at the Victorian auction, and Taxi sold for $2000 – more than double the reserve price. He was bought by BL Pastoral Company from Holbrook in New South Wales. They had been very keen to bid for the dog.

'I knew he was a good dog, but I was surprised by what was paid for him,' Rachael says. She is now keeping an online diary on her website featuring the training of Rousie, who is the Treasures' next Casterton Auction dog.

But life on the farm continues. A growing family, dogs to breed and train.

Rachael still has many goals ahead for her dogs. 'I want to do trialling with dogs. I would also like another breeding bitch and to be able to work with another breeder. I want to have an influence on farmers, teaching them to treat their dogs right.'

The day before they had left for Queensland Rachael had bought a pup from Paul McPhail's Kelpie Stud. Beloka Gippy is the foundation bitch for Rachael and John's Castleburn Kelpie & Border Collie Stud. They are committed to supplying well-bred dogs and to influencing farmers' training techniques. 'I want to help people train them positively and kindly.'

Her goal has won her a $10 000 bursary as the 2007 Tasmanian Rural Woman of the Year to create an e-book and dog training DVD to help people not only train their dogs but to tap into a network of Australian breeders and dog educators via the web. Rachael had seven dogs when I visited, including a Jack Russell called Indi, because she comes 'indi' house and sits under the desk while Rachael writes.

'My first dog was Dougall, a "giveaway" border collie advertised in the paper in Orange, New South Wales. He was sired by a good dog and he was my companion for over eight years. He was a legend on every level. He was a complete nut case, but a perfect gentleman. He used to go everywhere with me and sat underneath my desk at the ABC or in the studio. He used to travel in the glass lift at ABC Southbank in Melbourne. He used to work to the point of exhaustion. He was a high-jump champion and won so much money at competitions that he fed all the other dogs for two years. He died two years ago, when he was eight and a half years old. I still miss him and think of him every day.'

Rachael and I went for a walk to let the dogs off for a run. Seven excited and curious dogs raring to go play, round up sheep – and run. Gippy, Diamond, Alfred, Gibbo, Harvey, Chamois and Bitty (or Lil Bit) were all very excited to be off for a run and a play and to be able to check out the new bloke (me) with their 'mum'.

After a photo shoot with Rachael and her dogs, we drive to her parents' farm nearby with two of her best dogs. Rachael had to round up a flock of sheep into a yard. As she wanders off with her two dogs, it is obvious she is very comfortable working with them. Within minutes they have the sheep yarded and they are in the groove, working and loving every minute of it. They are bred to work.

Far too soon it is time for me to head off, and we promise to catch up again. I had a long drive ahead of me to get to Devonport and load my ute on board the *Spirit of Tasmania* for overnight sailing to Melbourne.

At the time I wrote in my notes that 'Rachael has many goals with her farming, her dogs and her writing. I leave knowing that with her determination, skill and dedication she would succeed at whatever she tries.'

She followed her first successful novel with *The Stockmen* in 2004. It is a book that moves between the present and the past, back as far as the 1850s, and it delves into the kelpie dog history in Victoria's western district. This is interwoven with Rachael's vivid representation of life in the bush today, with ute shows, pubs, country music, stockmen – and dogs, a life she writes about with great knowledge. Seems she did listen to the saying about writing what you know.

'Whilst the book is based on the actual life of Jack Gleeson, I'm a fiction writer, not a historian,' Rachael is quick to point out. Jack Gleeson is credited with the unusual contribution to Australian bush life of developing a breed of dog – and her book recognises 'his part in giving us that magic creature, the Australian working kelpie dog'. It is a book that immediately engaged readers, and many young country people relate to the life Rachael writes so well about. Rachael's latest novel, *The Rouseabout*, was published in 2007 and soared straight to the bestseller lists. Many people say it's her best book yet.

So what else does a bestselling author from the Tasmanian bush do in her life? Rachael lives it: dog trials, dog auctions, clearing sales, cattle and sheep sales, mountain cattlemen get-togethers, droving cattle in the High Plains or driving a family support vehicle. As John is a farrier, they both also attend shows and country events with their own horses, dogs and book displays. All this and much more make up part of the life of this Tasmanian bushie. I just call her a spunky mum.

By the time she is an old, grey-haired lady with dozens and dozens of books to her name and sitting on her verandah in her RM Williams boots, overlooking her dynasty, I hope she can look back on a life of love and passion for all that she wants. On her tombstone they can simply add that she was a talented Australian writer, farmer, dog trainer and much more, who 'jumped into life – boots 'n' all'.

See www.rachaeltreasure.com

The Chandelier Man

JIM, JUDY & JAMES ROWE

'PEOPLE UNDERSTOOD THE VALUE OF GOOD CRYSTAL CHANDELIERS.
THEY WERE INVESTING IN THE FUTURE; THEY KNEW THEIR
CHANDELIERS WOULD ACCRUE IN VALUE FOR FUTURE GENERATIONS:
THEY WERE A FAMILY HEIRLOOM.'

I was out of town on a road to another tiny village, the paddocks were all dry and it was a too warm day. The sign on the
gate said *Waratah Park*. Soon James Rowe and I were inside
the home he shares with his two aunts – Judy and Rose. I didn't
meet them until James and I returned from his shed – the
shed where his father had worked until his death in 2003. His
father, Edward, was known only as Jim, or in business as 'the
Chandelier Man'. When I met James's aunt Judy she referred
to father and son as Big Jim and Little Jim.

When we retreated inside again Judy went off to make a
morning cup of tea while James and I sat in the lounge and
talked. Soon I heard that Judy was also part of the Chandelier
Man business. She had worked on chandeliers for forty years.
She was 'the chandelier woman', but unassumingly, she said

she was just the back end of her brother's business, and that nephew James knew as much about the business as she did.

Both Judy and Big Jim were born in New Zealand. Their mother was Australian and their father was a New Zealander. Jim was born in 1924, and in 1956 the family moved to Melbourne to live. Both Jim and Judy worked at Myer. Jim's work in the lighting department gave him an idea. Many wealthy customers wanted to buy individually styled chandeliers, and also wanted people to clean and repair them. Jim decided he would become that man. He knew nothing about it, but decided he would learn.

At the time the family all lived at Upwey, and as they didn't own a car, Jim would get on the train with a ladder and a bucket-load of cleaning gear and travel down to Melbourne. He would wander around the wealthy suburbs of Toorak and South Yarra, looking for work cleaning chandeliers. Soon, word of mouth spread that there was a chandelier man who was willing to clean the delicate objects, and Jim gradually built up a business. He never advertised. As the business grew, it was decided to move home to Caulfield to be closer to work. He bought a Ford Prefect car, which he hand-painted blue and added roof racks for his ladders. Young James remembers how each night after dark his father, grandmother, aunt Judy, brother Terry and he would all pile into the little Ford and drive around Toorak and South Yarra looking into homes to see if chandeliers were burning brightly in the windows. They'd jump out and put the business card in the mailbox and wait for business to come. Soon, Jim was repairing chandeliers as well as cleaning them, even though he had to teach himself how. Judy left Myer to work with her brother, and they got in touch with crystal manufacturers overseas to get their catalogues and price lists. They then started importing what they needed into Australia. Much of it was Czechoslovakian and Austrian crystal. Jim had the brass frames made locally to fit his design. Jim also started to design individual chandeliers. Finally, they moved to Kooyong, right opposite the famed tennis courts, where there was a spare shop window for him to display his work. There was a room above as well which was used for storage. The Chandelier Man was well and truly in a specialised business.

When the Capitol Theatre in Melbourne was being renovated the 15-foot high candelabra was smashed by bricks as the workmen did their job. It ended up being stored at the Chandelier Man shop. The brass frame alone weighed 1 tonne and each arm coming from the centrepiece had a complete chandelier on the end itself. These were special candelabra – only twenty-two of them were ever made by the Baccarat company, only five survived the two world wars, one was in a casino in Monte Carlo and two were here in Australia. It was Jim and Judy's job to restore it back to its full glory, which they did but sadly it went back into storage and Jim never got to see it standing again. They had originally been built in 1888–89 for the Paris Exposition. Jim even drew diagrams showing how to assemble the tens of thousands of pieces that made up the full item.

'To work on them was really something; you got to really appreciate the magnificent workmanship,' said Judy. 'All beautiful solid crystal, every piece only fitted into the spot it was made for. We assembled one in the showroom. It was so big that when we put it together it was too tall for the downstairs room, so the top section we assembled in the upstairs room. It was French empire-style, very early Georgian with embossed chains and the prisms were hand-cut crystal. A magnificent piece.' Now, many years later, the candelabra are finally on display at the National Gallery of Victoria in St Kilda Road, Melbourne.

Jim and Judy worked from when the business was registered in 1963 until 2003, when Jim became very ill and died. It was forty years of painstaking and exacting work. 'Jim and I made a living from it; for me, it was the satisfaction of knowing I could do it, working on machines polishing and making and doing something that was special. I enjoyed the quality of old things – learning to work on beautiful old things is very satisfying. Challenging but rewarding. We were both self-taught. We gathered all the books we could find from the library, but they were mainly on gem cutting, which is a lot different.

'Jim was friends with a Czech designer called Jan Korinek, he did a lot of importing and assembling of pre-designed chandeliers, but Jim was keen to design individual pieces. We wrote to European – mainly West German and Austrian – crystal manufacturers and we got the crystal from them in rough cut form and worked from there.'

Judy went to make another cup of tea for us, and so I decided to ask James about his life. Judy returned briefly to show me an entry in a dictionary. 'Candelabrum' is singular, and 'candelabra' is the plural, and is described as a large branched candlestick. Good to know I got it right. 'I learn something new everyday,' as my ninety-five year-old grandmother used to say to me.

What has led James to become the next Chandelier Man? 'I worked with Dad and Judy in the shop when I left school, before I finally left for north Queensland – Cairns – and then I worked all over the place. I went to Coober Pedy as an opal digger and tow-truck driver, then to Boulder-Kalgoorlie in the mines and then followed the seasonal fruit picking from Queensland to Victoria each year – grapes, tomatoes, cherries and such. After that I went commercial fishing for coral trout off the Barrier Reef. Then between 1966 and 1974 I was a stockman on stations and spent between '74 and '86 doing seasonal work between Bowen in Queensland, where I lived, and down south. Then I was permanently on a farm in Bowen, before selling insurance for a couple of years around west Queensland, in the old spots I had previously worked, as well as in places like Townsville, Ingham, Cammoweal and many more. It was the cause of my marriage bust up: I was never home. When you travel in the outback you met a lot of fantastic people, eh?'

I said I knew he was a Queenslander because his sentences finished with 'eh?', which they are prone to do up there – eh? The Territorians are the same. James was born in New Zealand when his parents and grandparents lived over there. 'I call myself an Australian and then a Queenslander.'

'I went across to Western Australia to the Kimberley and worked on the building of the El Questro resort. The plant operator went walkabout, so I ended up having a go at the heavy equipment, driving a traxcavator with a clam bucket. I also drove a superlift truck. I stayed on and then they asked me to also be a fishing guide for them, as I had been involved in Queensland sport fishing for fourteen or fifteen years.

'El Questro is a great place now, the tourist resorts sits 50 feet above the water on a cliff. The first 6 feet in depth of the waters are really warm, and then you hit the cold waters, which are freezing. The weather was so hot we used to jump off the cliff at the end of the day, and the only way out was to swim 100 yards downstream, past the cliff to a pump station. There was always a salt-water crocodile watching on the other side of the river, but he must have thought it too hot to chase us. I was there in 1990, and it was a great time. I used to go out with a chopper pilot and we'd go fishing in remote spots and catch barramundi, but with both of us on board the little Robinson-22 helicopter we couldn't carry too many fish. With the weather being so hot, the chopper could only just fly as it was. They don't fly as good in that weather. I was making fishing lures out of old bumper bars and they sold really well, highly polished and they worked well, so I headed off to Darwin to sell more, but it had changed so much. I first went there in 1974, two weeks prior to Cyclone Tracy, but now it is totally different, so I headed off to the Wyndham as I knew I'd get a job at the meat works. When I got there I learnt it had burnt down six years before. I was then in Kununurra looking for work and I got a job as a rouseabout, labouring, and ended up driving a road train and a grader.

'After that, I came to live with Dad and Judy for a year, then I went back to Cairns and started as a rouseabout in a car-yard for a few years until they closed. By then I had a Motor Dealers' licence and sold cars on a small lot until 2004. Then I came here to live with Judy to look at restarting the Chandelier Man business.'

Judy rejoined us and we discussed various aspects of the business. James is lucky in that he has learnt a lot from both his father and aunt and now with her interest they can resurrect the Chandelier Man (and woman).

James has already made a prototype crystal chandelier for motor-homes. Owners of half-million-dollar specially built motor-homes appreciate quality. James's design is made from high-quality crystals, which are secure and don't wave about like normal ones hanging from ceilings. These are going to be small wall-lights and flat and domed ceiling lights. I had a good look at one of the wall lights and James is certainly on to a good idea and one that could well and truly get the business going again. But it will have its challenges. Nowadays there are no brass manufacturers left in Australia; the last one closed the year before last. All the brass for the type of work James does will have to be imported; it's limited in size and there are many grades of brass. As Judy said, the Chandelier Man business only ever used top-quality material and would never use anything less than the best. James continues, 'I am now in the planning stages and trying to get all the material I want, and I'm looking to re-establish it if people want it. We're now only doing personal repairs and special commission jobs. I would no longer travel to clean them; most of the work is to be done here.'

When James gets his motor-home chandeliers off the ground he would like to travel to motor-home shows and get-togethers all over Australia; he could think of nothing better than travelling and selling his work to appreciative buyers. The business also needs other people, and James is looking for the right person to assist, probably a retired person who likes working from home.

'Judy is a great pinner – every crystal had a tiny hole in it and wire needed to be threaded through it to hold it to the frame or another piece of crystal. Very exacting work. That was her specialty, and it's a difficult job. Judy never used a magnifying glass – she had patience, a steady hand and good eyes. Judy not only hand-made the pins, she also installed them. Long-nose pliers that had the end ground down and shaped into a fine length were one of her main tools of the trade.'

The shed that Jim Rowe worked in now holds a huge collection of crystal material of all shapes, sizes and ages. It's full of boxes of this and that, and many of the shelves are dusty – James has some tidying up to do before he gets back into full production. We look at many different pieces and James explains where they fit and how old they are; I am amazed at the beauty of individual pieces. His father used to buy old candelabra, gasoliers and chandeliers in the early days to build up stock and the collection is amazing.

I have three old chandeliers in a cupboard at home and I forgot to bring them up to show James, but I will soon. One I know is pretty old and made entirely of crystal. The other two are on brass frames. All need restoration.

I was keen to know all about crystals. James spent quite a long time showing me and telling me about them.

'Old crystals had their tiny holes cut in from the back, half-way through a crystal and then down from the top to meet. Often the holes don't entirely match up. Later-model ones usually just have a tiny hole cut straight through from the back to the front when made in the mould.

'A raw prism is made by molten lead crystal being poured into a mould and allowed to cool. Usually the lead content was between 18 and 22 per cent, but most of the cheaper ones have a higher lead content. Lead brings out the light in a crystal. Many of the crystal manufacturers have secrets as to the content ratio of the sand, silica, potash, and lead oxide compositions. Once the crystal cools in the mould, it shrinks and the flat surface in the mould becomes dimpled. The cutting or grinding is done on a diamond wheel or cork wheel (black cork is an abrasive, yellow is less so). Each piece is individually facet-cut, using cerium oxide for the final polish. It is known as jewellers' rouge. Doing one crystal prism usually takes an average of about ten minutes. Dad and Judy made hanging chandeliers, wall brackets, flush-fitting ones for low ceilings, candelabra, candlesticks, gasoliers – anything to do with crystal lights.'

The walls of their home are covered with all sorts of crystal, a cabinet has a collection of unusual prisms, and the walls also have many of Judy's artworks – she is a specialist painter of horses.

'Dad was a jockey in New Zealand, and Grandfather had coach and harness horses, and bred horses. We were always around horses. When Jim and I came here in 1987, we were retired but still doing some work. We moved to the country so we could have horses; Jim was a registered owner-trainer. That photo on the wall is our first winner – Nilbasca – who won his first race at St Arnaud in 1989. He loved the dry and hated rain or water. He would run straight back into his shed if it rained. Well, it rained for three days before his first race, and here he was churning up mud as he galloped to win the race. It was such a thrill for us.'

I wanted to know more of Judy's art – she is a very talented lady – but we got side-tracked and went back to talking chandeliers for a while.

'Here, we were approached by the shire tourism people and asked if we'd like to have tourist buses stop here to see what we did. So, from 1997 we took it on, and we also trained some local people in how to cut and polish crystal and how to make candlesticks. We had five women and two men as part of a training program. I also taught them how to paint on crystal and gave them confidence to have a go. A couple of the women carried on with it.'

So how did Judy become such a fine artist?

'She is a very talented lady,' says Rose, her sister, who came from New Zealand to live with them. Rose is a bright, cheery lady, who says she has no talent, but she is a happy lady – interested and interesting. Judy says Rose has talent but never worried about using it. Rose just laughs. Judy then explains how it all happened.

'I was self-taught, basically; I got the books from the library at school. Mum was a gifted drawer of horses; she'd criticise my work and tell me what was wrong with it. My grandmother gave me a tin paint-box, which I still have. A friend of hers left it with her when he went off to World War One, he specialised in painting flowers. He never came home – killed in the war. When I showed interest in drawing Grandmother gave me his paint tin with all the materials inside. My brother Jim many years later prevailed upon me to put a painting into the *Herald Sun* Art Show in Melbourne, and so I had to rush around and get one finished. I was over the moon when it was one of the first sold, and I got £25 for it. I feel it gave me assurance and confidence to do more. People then started to ask me to paint dogs, horses and such, but it was mainly just a hobby as crystal work was the main thing because it was our business.'

Judy combined her talent as a chandelier maker with art; she started to paint individual tiny artworks on to single flat crystals: beautiful tiny scenes of birds, motorbikes, and a series of highly detailed historic horses with men in uniform. She did a lot of research into military uniforms. How she manages such detail in miniature is amazing. She reads a lot and studies as well. She is a perfectionist with her work. I think it comes from her many years of doing fine work on high quality pieces.

'People understood the value of good crystal chandeliers.

They were investing in the future; they knew their chandeliers would accrue in value for the future generations: they were a family heirloom. It was for their own personal enjoyment and pleasure of a possession to pass it on to family members. A good chandelier will last hundreds of years and may have done so, not the cheap ones like those available now from South America, Europe and Asia, but the good ones of old.

'A small five-arm hand-cut crystal chandelier is worth about $3000 upwards. Candlesticks range from $250 to $800. One of the gasoliers we worked on took eight months to do and it was worth about $40 000. One of the dearest we made was for a stately home in Melbourne and was worth about $60 000.' I was shown a folder containing photos of many of the chandeliers they'd worked on, but as Judy said, 'I can't let you use photos of them as they are in private homes and we respect their privacy.' Fair enough, too.

'The hardest one to construct had to match an oval ceiling. When making an oval-shaped chandelier, the most difficult thing is to get all the proportions right, and to ensure everything matches as they reduce down. They really are a headache, real terrors to work with.'

So, after forty years of working with her brother, Judy now will be beside her nephew James as he takes on more work and hopefully continues to expand the role of the Chandelier Man. If readers want to have a look at an example of their work, they can go to Werribee Park Mansion near Melbourne. It is open to the public, and at the top of the stairs is a magnificent chandelier that has had the talented hands of Jim and Judy Rowe turn it into a wonderful piece. Their work will live on in many homes – both grand and everyday.

As I prepared to journey on, Judy handed me a small parcel

wrapped in tissue paper. It was a small frame with a flat crystal, and painted on it were two tiny birds on a flowering branch. How lucky I am to get to put that on the sideboard at home; it will always remind me of the Chandelier Woman and her talented brother and nephew.

Peter the Ploughman

PETER KELM

'I'VE GOT THE IDEAS IN MY HEAD, BUT WHAT YEAR
THEY GET DONE I'VE GOT NO IDEA.'

It was a warm day and I'd spent time out photographing the dingo-dog-rabbit-proof fence. Not the one in Western Australia that was the basis of the movie. It wasn't the smaller one in South Australia either; it wasn't the dingo-dog fence, which is the longest fence in the world. (Even though the signs say the Western Australian rabbit-proof fence is the longest, it isn't. There are numerous fences that claim to be something special.) The fence I was photographing is now almost non-existent, except for a few small preserved remnants and the memorials erected saying where it once was. This dingo-dog-rabbit-proof fence is near Jeparit in Victoria. I also photographed it on the Calder Highway near Wycheproof.

The plaque near Jeparit on the Rainbow Road at Geppert's Gate – 'Gateway to the Mallee' – has colourful murals and two memorials – one to the fence and one to surveyor Tom H. Turner, who in 1884 attempted to survey the 36 degree parallel of latitude from the 142 degree meridian of longitude to the South Australian border, a distance of 93 kilometres. A post refers to 36S 142E. A sign opposite points out the direction of the 'line of dingo-dog-rabbit-proof fence'.

The other memorial on the Calder Highway near Wycheproof is the corner of the Calder Highway and Dog Netting Road. The stone memorial with plaque says it commemorates the 1885 construction of the 'dog-netting fence', running from Tyntynder (near Swan Hill) to the South Australian border – a distance of 204 miles. The memorial says the fence is designed to 'prevent wild dogs and other vermin from entering the farm lands to the south.' Whatever it says about the fence there isn't much of it left, and now little is recorded anywhere about it.

What has all this got to do with the story of Peter the ploughman? Absolutely nothing, except it wasn't far from here that he farmed land with his parents, and left his mark on the land. It also gives you a glimpse of local history that can be found just by driving around and taking time out. I've found all sorts of stuff over the years.

I was filling in time as I was wandering in search of new stories, new things to photograph and places to see. I often just go off wandering between setting up interviews. On this day I had some free time and I was enjoying finding new things. It's just part of my job. I love learning. Little did I know that I would end up interviewing a man who made headlines many years ago, and it would be just because by chance I drove up his street and past his place, before doing a U-turn. I instantly recognised a statue in his front yard. I'd seen a photo in the *Weekly Times*, and had torn it out to put into one of my many files to follow up. And here many years later, I was sitting right outside the gate of Peter the ploughman. My day off was finished and it was time to get back to work.

Peter Kelm would be the first to agree he is a bit of a bush dag, and he's not afraid to speak his mind. He could even be called a bush ratbag or eccentric. He'd laugh at any tag. He likes a good laugh and hopes others can understand his weird sense of humour. Not all would agree on his musings, but that's life. He also likes to promote his hometown.

Many people would like the opportunity to really stick it up politicians. In 1986 Peter created his own chance to voice his objection to the then prime minister, Bob Hawke, but little did he realise at the time he would gain national attention for his comments. Fed up with a government that didn't seem to realise how serious things were in the bush, farmer Peter jumped on his Ford 7000 tractor one morning with disc plough attached and headed out. In 50-foot long letters he ploughed a message across one of the farm paddocks for all to see – 'HAWK FEATHERS HIS OWN NEST AND SHITS IN OURS'. He also added 'CUT FUEL TAXES'. He later scarified the letters.

'People asked me how I did it so well. I just used my instinct – didn't use plans or stakes – I just wrote out the message on a piece of paper and then went and did it. I didn't tell Mum or anyone. They'd reckon it a waste of diesel for the tractor. It took me half a day to do it. I left the E off Hawke in case he tried to sue me or something. Later on the media talked me into adding it on though.'

Peter later added other messages such as 'FAIR GO' and 'I SUPPORT RURAL VICTORIA', and even added a ploughed picture of a windmill. The media loved it, and newspapers and television showed his work for the whole of Australia to see.

'The local CB radios in the district didn't stop for a while – people had plenty to say.'

Even ten years later the *National Farmer* magazine ran a small article titled 'The Hawk's flown but the feathers are still in the nest,' in which Peter commented that although ten years had passed, very little had changed: life was still tough for farmers.

Peter Kelm grew up on the farm that his grandfather, Adolph Kelm, started many years ago at Tarranyurk near Jeparit in the north-west of Victoria. His parents, Harold and Una, took over the wheat and barley farm and stayed there until it was sold in 1988. 'We had pigs but I got rid of them. I worked hard for many years, and have always had help from my brothers and friends in the area. I worked hard with Dad, carting hay and superphosphate bags in shearing sheds and off the back of trucks. That's why I have back and knee problems now. I'm on a pension.'

'Once, a newspaper person was in the district, looking for people and crops to photograph. A neighbour told him that he had something better to show him, and he flew over the place in a plane from Horsham – and then my work was plastered all over papers around Australia. I had about six radio stations ring me for interviews as well. Even Debbie Byrne from the *Mike Willesee Show* on TV came and did a story about it. Lots of people just laughed, some got upset but I didn't worry about them. Then I sold the farm and Mum and I moved into town. She still lives nearby. I bought this house and have been here ever since.'

Not content to live anonymously in a town street, Peter decided to continue making his thoughts known. He laughs at his own jokes and loves to tinker about with welding machines. 'I can't do it much now – my knees make it hard to walk, and

I'm on a walking stick.' His mind is still keen though.

'My grandfather was a blacksmith, and I was mainly a self-taught welder, but I did courses at Horsham TAFE doing mig welding, bronzing, aluminium and cast iron welding. I passed it all okay. I started making steel sculptures from bits from around the farm and the tip. I like to show people my character. I like to help put Jeparit on the map.'

That he has done, and his garden of weird and wonderful sculptures has appeared on TV on *Postcards* and *Location, Location,* and has featured in an article in Jennifer Isaac's book *Quirky Gardens,* as well as in papers like the *Weekly Times* and the *Australasian POST.* The whole outside of Peter's house is covered in fantastic bits and pieces: tin sculptures of planes and rockets on the roof, and heavy-welded sculptures in the front yard, like Ned Kelly and the dog Scooby Doo. An alligator sculpture is a favourite of his.

'I got first prize with a carved wooden alligator at a couple of shows, but it got eaten by white ants in the end. I've made a motorbike with pedals, windmills, ploughs and a whole lot more. I like to add my own thoughts and comments, and so the outside walls are covered with funny and often rude quotes from magazines, books and such. Mum often says "You shouldn't have that one up there!"'

Peter laughs a lot and can see the funny side of his character.

'I've got plenty of wood drying out, waiting for me to start work on it,' he laughs. 'I'd like to build an aeroplane; I've got the motor from a Victa lawnmower, and I've got the wheels. It's been on the brain for a while.' We wander around looking at his work and reading the many messages on the front wall of his house. Messages like the following:

LOST
CAT – three legs, blind in left eye, large scar on throat,
bullet wound behind right ear, left ear missing,
tail broken in three places, no teeth,
recently castrated.
Answers to the name of LUCKY.

Other notes on the front wall of the house include:

MY WIFE DOES BIRD IMITATIONS –
SHE WATCHES ME LIKE A HAWK.

A WOMAN LED ME DOWN THE ROAD TO DRINK –
I NEVER WROTE TO THANK HER.

I'M AN AUSSIE AND PROUD OF IT.

SAVE WATER – DRINK BEER.

SEX KILLS – DIE HAPPY.

And there's even one for the New Zealanders – A KIWI SHEEP FARMER WAS COUNTING HIS SHEEP . . . 902, 903, 904, HELLO DARLING, 906, 907 . . .

And some I don't think I'd better put in print here!

I mentioned about all the sculptures in the garden, but I particularly wanted to know about the motorbike in the front yard. I'd said I'd seen it in the *Weekly Times* years ago. He laughs, 'Yeah, that's stupid, that. I just grabbed all the pieces from the tip, did it about ten years ago. I thought adding a set of pushbike pedals was a bit of a laugh.'

I wondered when he would add another sculpture to the garden.

'I've got the ideas in my head, but when and what year they get done I've got no idea.'

Life is what you make it, and Peter doesn't mind being a bit of a character – so long as it promotes his home town and gets people interested. Too many people in too many streets live life afraid to be heard, but Peter likes to pass on his comments, and hopefully make people put a smile on their dial.

Nothing wrong with that – smiles use less muscles than a frown.

scenic illusionist

KAREN TROTT

'EVEN THOUGH I DON'T LIKE HEIGHTS, I WAS PAINTING ON THE DOME CEILING ON SCAFFOLDING THAT DIDN'T HAVE CROSS-BRACING AND THAT SWAYED BACK AND FORTH.'

You know you're pretty good at what you do when you are asked to work for people from all over the world. From Singapore to Ukraine, from Disney to Harvey Norman, many have used the services of Karen Trott. She lives amongst the sugar gum trees on three acres surrounded by wide-open farming lands, a quiet retreat not far from Geelong and between the You Yang Ranges and Brisbane Ranges National Park.

Her quarter-horse Hollywood Irrepressible (nicknamed Dakota) is content to lie underneath some wattle trees, oblivious to me taking photographs.

Horses have been a part of Karen Trott's life ever since she was given her first Shetland pony called Pearl, when she was just four years of age. Between the ages of ten to fourteen, Karen appeared in the national television series *The Terrible*

Ten. It was filmed near Mount Macedon, where she lived on a farm.

'They wanted me in it for my horse-riding abilities more than my acting prowess,' laughs Karen. Since then Karen, or KT as she's known, has always had horses. In later years she 'helped in the local pony-club scene'; she used to compete at shows, and has done quarter-horse events and more. Her mother and stepfather sold their property next to the famous Hanging Rock and now live on a property in Queensland training harness horses. Karen is a member of the Quarter-horse Association. Her days of riding are limited now as her work keeps her busy.

Born in Kyneton Hospital fifty-plus years ago, Karen grew up at Macedon, north of Melbourne. She went to school at Macedon and later in Kyneton, before going to university, spending three years in the early 1970s gaining her Bachelor of Fine Arts (Painting and Printmaking). It was during this time she realised her love of doing work on a large scale. She decided to move into scenic art rather than fine art. It is an interest that has carried on for many years. Although she had the talent and the qualifications, Karen found it hard to get work at the time. She did the rounds of television stations, theatre companies and such to no avail.

'In those days scenic art wasn't regarded as women's work. They'd say you can't do it, as you'd have to climb ladders and there are no facilities for women, and all the other stories to put you off. In the end I went into the Melbourne Theatre and worked for nothing for six months. Six months with no pay, just so I could prove I could do it, and I got some lousy jobs, but ended up getting a full-time job with them for the next five and a half years.

'Then I decided I wanted to try doing freelance work, but continued to do some work for the Melbourne Theatre Company part time for two years. I then worked for the Victorian State Opera doing all the stage backdrops for various productions. Later I started doing work in TV for both Channel 9 and Channel 10, doing a lot of the sets for shows like *The Paul Hogan Show, Sale of the Century, The Don Lane Show* and others. Later I was the head scenic artist on *Water Under the Bridge*, a mini-series starring Robyn Nevin, John Howard, Jackie Weaver, Briony Behets and others I can't remember.'

By that time Karen's reputation for large-scale scenic art was established, and in 1985 she accepted a job in Singapore, working with an American design company for eight months, creating a huge underwater theme for the Atlantis Night Club, which also entailed doing sculptured ceilings. 'I worked with some amazingly talented Americans on that job, and made some long-term friends as a result. While there I ended up also designing special costumes for all the staff. When I returned to Australia eight months later, I was keen to develop more in the architectural field. I took on a job for Jag clothing, doing the interiors for their headquarters in Richmond, and many inter-state outlets, painting the reception area, and owner/fashion designer Adele Palmer's office.'

While doing all sorts of freelance work, Karen was also employed by the Playbox Theatre to paint their on-stage sets, and they also commissioned her to do a large oil painting to hang in the theatre.

The movies are all about creating illusions. You see a scene of what looks like a mansion filled with antique furniture. Chances are it's either foam, fibreglass or cheap wood, but it is people like Karen Trott who can turn them into a piece that looks hundreds of years old, like an expensive antique. The movie *Street Hero*, with Sigrid Thornton, was a classic example of Karen's ability to create something from next to nothing. The film included much of Karen's scenic and set art, including a huge mural for just one scene.

'They finished filming one day, and said to me that they wanted a reproduction of the *Last Supper* to go on the wall behind a dinner table. It had to be ready to be filmed in a scene at 8 a.m. the next morning! I worked all through the night and finished the 30 foot by 14 foot painting in time. From there I took on all sorts of private commissions on both the inside and outside of all sorts of buildings and private homes, mainly huge mansions in Melbourne's wealthy suburbs, such as Toorak and Brighton.'

Karen spent time over three and a half years on one huge mansion, Holm Park. Much of the interior Karen embellished in 23-karat gold decorative finishes. She also worked on a commission for Lady Susan Renouf, a well-known Melbourne socialite. Karen's painting techniques create beautiful aged looks – French provincial, Tuscan and other styles. She specialises in work like gold-leaf, patinas and techniques no longer common. She can create marbled walls with her paintbrush, and any number of other special effects. In short, she can take a bit of cheap furniture made from pine or craftwood and make it look like an ancient relic or antique discovered in some long-lost city. She creates illusions with walls, ceilings and furniture.

'I sort of came full circle because I ended up back with the Australian Ballet Company doing scenic art, and then I did the many gilded pieces for the *Sound of Music* stage production, starring Lisa McCune. I did more theatrical work and then

went back to doing private commissions, and that seems to be the blend of work now – both private commissions and theatrical work. At one stage I did special painted finishes and themes in various departments, and also on outside walls of about a dozen Harvey Norman stores all over Sydney and Melbourne, as well as in country New South Wales and Queensland.

Karen is a specialist and her home has become her main workshop. 'As much as possible now I like to bring work home and do it at my pace.' When I arrived to see her she had 'just undercoated some crappy kitchen cupboards and drawers made from craftwood'. She was turning them into a French provincial-style kitchen. On the cold cement floor of her workshop, which is covered with all types of paint and brushes and materials that are part of her trade, Karen goes about her work quietly and with precision. She has done it all before – all the preparation of the surfaces and laying down the undercoats. In a few days it will be complete and she will deliver it all in the back of her Falcon RTV ute, ready to be installed in a city mansion.

I have seen much of KT's work: she did a home near where I live in special finishes, adding many thousands of dollars to the home's value. Her many portfolios show off her talent. I am going to commission her to do some work myself, not for any fancy French provincial styling or gold-leaf embossing, but for an Australian-themed painting to suit my own style. I have every confidence she will create the look I want; she has the experience and the talent.

In late 2003 Karen was approached by the same project manager she worked for in Singapore to work on a project in Korea. She was recommended as a specialist scenic artist for a major project, and this meant four months away from home for Karen. 'I flew to Korea to live one and a half hours south of Seoul, at Aiinsworld, a purpose-built tourist theme-park, which is made up of 56 acres of buildings and other attractions built by two American companies for the Korean owners. Half a million US dollars a day was being spent on the park.'

It is promoted as the theme park where you can 'travel the world in a day'. All the attractions are scale copies of the most famous landmarks around the world. Australia is represented by the Sydney Opera House. The total number of buildings in the complex is eighty, and they include the Eiffel Tower, the Arc de Triomphe, the Paris Opera House, the Louvre, Notre Dame, and many South American attractions such as Machu Picchu. There are also a lot of American buildings on site – the Empire State Building, the Rockefeller Centre, the White House and more. Mt Kilimanjaro also makes an appearance, and includes a sound and light show of volcanic noise, smoke and such. A space shuttle is also there, complete with a sophisticated sound show. A specialist from America was in charge of all the very high-tech special effects, including the lighting for all the buildings. Other features include the Great Wall of China, Vatican City, the British Houses of Parliament, Red Square in Moscow, and the Taj Mahal in India. Behind the buildings, the landscape consisted of ten long walls spread out, each being 60 metres long and 8 metres high. 'They were a blank space and I was in charge of turning them into beautiful scenes that complemented the buildings. Some students and I had to create everything – from intricate French painting techniques to wide-ranging scenes of city and natural landscapes.'

Karen was in charge of local art students – between six and fourteen students each day – most spoke little or no English. Her two local bosses were educated in New York and Newcastle,

New South Wales, and so they had to be Karen's interpreters. Sourcing materials for the huge job was difficult, so in the end Karen arranged for some to be imported from Australia. She found learning Korean difficult, but said she soon learnt how to order a beer in Korean. The Korean owners thought the job would take about three weeks, but the American companies and Karen soon informed them just how long it would really take. Work was often on scaffolds high above the ground and meant working from 7 a.m. to 7 p.m., seven days a week in all sorts of weather. Earning big money means hard work, but Karen enjoys using her talents for big challenges.

Four months later the job was done for the tourists of the world to see and for the many local students to use, as it is also an educational resource. Karen returned to Australia, back to her normal commission and theatre work.

'My next overseas job came in 2006 when I left for the eastern side of Ukraine for three and a half months. I was working as part of a team on a private palace owned by the country's richest man, a mining magnate and owner of just about everything in the city, including a soccer team. He is so powerful he tried to secede from Ukraine and turn his city into his own country. The palace is having billions of dollars spent on it. All workers had to pass through his own private army and the security each day. Getting in and out of the palace was like it is in an airport – sniffer dogs and electronic surveillance. No items like cigarette lighters, mobile phones or cameras were permitted. I was part of a team of fourteen artists from Australia. Tradesmen doing marble work came from Turkey and Italy. All tradespeople were artisans in their fields. One plasterer was a female doctor who made more money doing the delicate plaster work than practising medicine.

'Over thirty gilders from Kiev were set the task of doing gold-leaf work. The gold leaf throughout the palace was extraordinary and took up many, many hundred of metres. In one room there were two tapestries worth over one million dollars each. Other rooms had rare Italian marble. I worked in the Grand Salon, a huge room with a three-storey high domed roof. Even though I don't like heights, I was painting on the dome ceiling on scaffolding that didn't have cross-bracing so it swayed back and forth. My work included painting a variety of architectural panels, floral arrangements and birds, as well as other decorative features.

'Once again language was a huge barrier as it is a non-English speaking place, however I found learning a little Russian easier than Korean. I love the challenge. Whilst the apartment I lived in looked modern, and had modern appliances and such on the inside, the exteriors of all buildings are owned by the government and look derelict, they're ruins with concrete cancer and a very dilapidated look. The government only turns the heating on from the power grid on certain days, regardless of the weather.'

After months away, in January 2007, Karen returned to Australia with work left in yet another part of the world to show off her talent. She was glad to come home to her beloved few acres, her ute, her horse Dakota, her precious cats – and her partner Russell, of course, who works as an engineer at Ford in Geelong, designing and building all sorts of vehicles but mainly working as the senior product engineer on the great Aussie ute.

Ford Geelong is the home of the Australian ute, designed and built there in 1934, but it was Geelong resident Lew Bandt who became famous for designing the first successfully mass-produced one-piece ute. Even Henry Ford affirmed the importance of the ute, dubbing it the 'kangaroo chaser', and building an American version, based on the Aussie design. Russell and his colleagues at Ford Geelong carry on the tradition set by designer Lew Bandt.

Russell has just added some major features to their home, which now await Karen's specialised talents to turn them into something magic with her brushes and paint. Like many of the talented people I've met, Karen's work is something you want to own.

She creates something from almost nothing. She wouldn't have it any other way.

Animal Antics

SARAH & CODY RAWSON-HARRIS
'GIVE THEM A LOT OF LOVE, TRUST AND RESPECT AND
THEY'LL GIVE YOU THE WORLD.'

Nowadays we see more and more movies that have animals as a major theme, whether they are animated shows like *Happy Feet* or have real, live animals specifically trained, such as in *Babe* and the recent *Charlotte's Web*. Who trains these amazing animals to do the sorts of tasks and antics they are asked to perform? Movie star animals have been around for almost as long as there have been films, so who trains the trainers? In the case of Cody Rawson-Harris, he didn't have to look far.

He grew up in movies, and both his parents, father Heath Harris and mother Ivana, have trained animals for many, many years. Their work is seen in Australian films such as *The Irishman*, *Phar Lap*, *Mad Max 3*, *The Man from Snowy River*, *We of the Never Never*, *Breaker Morant*, and heaps more, as well as commercials such as the *Marlboro Man* ads.

Cody and his wife, Sarah, have a farm next to Burkie, a mate of Mongrel and me. I travelled to Murchison in the Goulburn Valley of Victoria to spend some time with them. It was a hot day and underneath a large tree in the backyard that overlooks the creek we sat and had a chat. Being animal lovers they of course had their 'family' with them, including Ginger Meggs, the nine-year-old red heeler, Whoopie the four-year-old kelpie and Charlie Bird the crow, who is wild but is more at home flying around us and feeding before flying off to sit in a large monkey puzzle tree with a heap of short billed corellas. I would get to see the rest of the family later.

'I was born in Mona Vale, Sydney, in 1973 and my first appearance on the screen was when I was six years old. The movie was *The Earthling* with William Holden and I was the stand-in for Ricky Schroder,' says Cody. 'Between 1976 and 1989 we lived in the hills between Gloucester and Walcha on 600 acres, with no electricity and a heap of film animals. Later my parents' business evolved at Terrey Hills in Sydney: Dad did horse-breaking, saddler and riding school and the Marlboro commercials, and things grew. Mainly Dad was into training horses and Mum's main influence in training was with other animals like cows, kangaroos, emus, wombats and some horses. Heath Harris International supplied a lot of animals for the movies I worked for.

'After Mum and Dad divorced, I worked with Australian Movie Livestock with my mother on movies such as *Archer*, *Burke & Wills* (I was an extra on that one), *The Dirtwater Dynasty* and commercials. *Porno Girl* came later,' he says with a laugh. 'We also did *Star Runner* in New Zealand, then home to do *Quigley Down Under*, *Reckless Kelly*, with Yahoo Serious, and *Silver Brumby*.

'I started running my own jobs when I was nineteen. The first one was on *The New Adventures of Black Beauty*. Between 1993 and 1996 I did sixty-five episodes of the TV series of *The Man from Snowy River*, then the *On Our Selection* movie, and back to TV with work on episodes of *Blue Heelers* and other movies like *Welcome to Woop Woop*, which we did near Alice Springs. Then came a kids' show called *Thunderstone*, and *Noah's Ark* and *Moby Dick*. I did *Jack the Ripper* for US cable TV. I left the family business in 1999.

'I drove meat trucks for a year at Melton near Melbourne – totally different to working in the film industry. One day I was in Mt Eliza and running late and a flower truck was blocking the way. I met Sarah in the car park and the rest is history, as they say. But it took a while. I was also doing harness clinics at weekends at Dingley, and asked Sarah if she'd like to come out for a drink. It was only then we found out we were both into horses.

'One day out of the blue I got a call from America and was asked to train a team of four hackney horses for four months in Kentucky. When I got home Mum rang one day to ask if I would work on *Horses: The Story of Equus* for Imax. She was already working on *Kangaroo Jack* and so couldn't do it. Then I worked on some commercials – the *Uncle Sam* one and the now-famous *Antz Pants* one where they even had an ant-wrangling scientist who got the job of putting on and removing the ants from the young model's body.

'The *Snowy River* series took four years of my life, working in snow and freezing weather. I was just thrown into it and had to make it all happen. People think making movies and TV is glamorous but it's not; it's damned hard work.'

I asked Cody to name some of the actors he has worked with

over the years. I could add the ones he liked and the ones he didn't, but I won't. He is pretty casual about it all.

'Russell Crowe, Wendy Hughes, Lee Horsley, Hugh Jackman, Guy Pearce, Olivia Newton-John, Andrew Clarke, Jack Thompson, Dakota Fanning, Rod Taylor. I've been the double for Nicholas Cage, Brett Climo and many more.'

Cody's wife, Sarah Healey, was born in Prahran in 1974. Her parents, Glenys, and Davis had a flower-growing business for many years at Dingley. They also had a cattle farm at Mansfield.

'I went to Mentone Girls Grammar but left at age sixteen so I could go to Fish Creek to work with horse-breakers. I was always keen on horses. Then I was a vet nurse in Melbourne for two and a half years before going to Wagga Wagga – again working for a horse trainer, riding and breaking horses in. I craved knowledge and learnt as much as I could.

'In 1998 some friends in Wagga were talking about the US and they gave me a contact there. I worked in Lamar, Colorado with cutting horses for a year, and then I went to Longmont looking for work and so the story goes. I arrived there with $5 in my pocket. It was snowing as I walked into a bar; by the time I left I had a job as a barmaid. I then got a job breaking cutting horses in and starting two-year-olds and also worked with cattle. I was there for a year. Going to the US taught me a lot. I did a lot of growing up, believing in myself and learning to stand on my own. I was working sixteen hours a day, though, and I got burnt out. I did it tough but I learnt a lot. I travelled to Missouri, Nebraska and Wyoming, and then came home to Melbourne for six months before going to Benalla, breaking horses in for anyone who needed it.

'In 2000 I went back to Melbourne to help Dad with the

flower business. I did deliveries in the flower truck. That was how I met Cody.

'Mum and Dad are second-generation flower growers; they have a shop on the property and we've mainly grown lisianthus, carnations, chrysanthemums and freesias. The business mainly exported to Bulgaria, the US and Japan. Mum and Dad have worked very hard all their lives and it's great to see what they achieved, but sad to see the business now getting older as they do too.'

It was at this point that Roger the rooster decided to interrupt proceedings and with his two females in tow he walked past, letting us know he was about. Back to Sarah.

'Horses were all I did, and if I wasn't doing that then I wasn't happy. I've always had animals around me, like dogs. I learnt to ride when I was three on our great dane called Andy. I did it tough – no saddle. I owned my first horse at four years old. He was called Ben.'

When Sarah and Cody got together, Sarah had a 6-tonne Isuzu truck, which she bought off her father. Both she and Cody had a horse each and they trained three horses in a paddock at the flower farm. They added a bakery cart box on to the truck so they could move their horses about. Then they started Caballo Horse Transport. Things were tight. Cody didn't want to work at horse transport as a job, but it paid the bills, and the day they finished setting up their truck they got their first job. They also worked training horses for people. In November 2001 Cody did the stunt work on *Ponderosa*, directed by Australian Simon Wincer, and this was followed in early 2002 with training the stage coach team of horses on the movie *Ned Kelly*, which starred Heath Ledger. He was also the double for actor Orlando Bloom. It was during that time Sarah learnt how to teach a horse to get onto its mark – the exact spot the film director wanted an animal to stand. 'It changed my life,' says Sarah. The excitement of training animals for film was for her.

In October 2002 Cody and Sarah bought their farm: a run-down, overgrown old trotting place, which they share with their horses Tommi, Flea, Denny, Rodney, Windy and Dusty, and dogs Meggs, Whoopie, Ash and Sooty. 'When we first moved in we lived on two-minute noodles and were as happy as pigs in shit,' laughs Sarah. It was the start of a new life and a lot of hard work. Now their farm is a beautiful spot, set up with a huge indoor arena for training animals, a holiday cottage, new yards and lawns, and a look of permanence about it.

In May 2003 Sarah and Cody headed off to South Africa to train horses for the movie *Racing Stripes*, a ten-month shoot inland from Durban. 'It was a great experience,' says Sarah, 'but it's a hard place. We had eighty horses to handle. We learnt a lot, and had a good sense of our own worth – you get respect for what you do.

'During 2004 we broke in horses at home until we were asked to do a Qantas commercial at Falls Creek, and in November 2004 we went into pre-production for the movie *Charlotte's Web*: four months of training two horses and eleven sheep. Then we did filming between February and July 2005, which was fantastic. There were five US animal trainers, four other Aussie trainers and ourselves. There was a lot of politics involved with who did what, but we were very happy with the result. The US owner of those eleven sheep left them here with us now and hopefully they will be here permanently.'

The sheep were two-and-a-half-year-old border leicesters.

They were taken straight from a paddock and Sarah had three months to train them all to do exactly was required by the film makers. 'They were as wild as sheep can be, every sheep had a different personality, but I worked with them individually and then as a group. I taught them all the tricks required for the film and after eight weeks I had them ready to go on set, so I was happy. I kept going and taught them some other tricks as well,' says Sarah proudly.

Cody had horses in the film, and as usual one special one. 'Rodney, who I nicknamed Pod, is a big chestnut: 16 hands high with flashing white socks. He had worked with me on every job since he was a two-year-old on *Silver Brumby*. He is an utter gentleman.'

I was lucky enough to have my own private ringside show as Sarah and Cody introduced me to some of their animals. We entered the huge indoor arena not far from the house, and in came four of the sheep that were used in *Charlotte's Web*. Sarah immediately went into training mode and the sheep responded. Sheep opening gates with their noses; sheep walking in circles in harmony, sheep shaking hands and walking like a caballo horse with outstretched legs, sheep lying down next to Sarah, all four sheep walking up to a post and rail fence in unison and turning their heads the same way on command. All done with precision and quiet assurance – it was a joy to behold. Whoopie the kelpie would have loved to have rounded them up, but he knew better, and hid behind a post and kept a watchful eye on them.

After a great show with the sheep, Cody got Whoopie to do some tricks on two legs and some other manoeuvres, and then it was time to go to a paddock on the other side of the house to see Cody's horses. A simple call and four of them came running across the paddock. Cody wanted to show me what Rodney could do. All the horses knew something was up and wanted to join in and come out the gate, but it was Rodney's show this time, and soon they too stood and watched as Cody and Rodney did some tricks. Standing right beside Cody with my camera, I was amazed just how big a 16-hand horse is when it's raised up on its two hind legs. After some other impressive work, it was time to give Rodney a break and he walked with us quietly back to his mates in the paddock.

In 2005 Sarah and Cody were married in their garden, and the dogs were dressed with bow-ties, and the other animals mingled with the guests. The creek flooded a couple of days before the wedding and all looked great.

Almost time to go, and before we went to do some photographing, I wanted to know where they'd go from here. Cody has his ideas. 'We want to be respected for what we do with animals; we want to train and supply good quality animals and run our business, Film Livestock Australia Pty Ltd, the way it should be run – professionally and properly.'

This young couple have a real love of animals. They respect them and talk to and treat them as a real part of their family, not like a lot of brutal people who see animals just as money-spinners. What a great couple of trainers, and their animals are a magnificent bunch. Time, though, for me to leave, and I look forward to catching up with them again. I told them of a book I have on dog training which I used to train my kelpie Dusty to do all sorts of tricks, so next time I'll call in not only with the book, but with Dusty the wonder dog as well. He says he wants to be a movie star, too. After saying our goodbyes, I head off down a dusty road, contented with the fact that some animals used in movies are truly well looked after.

As Sarah sums it up, the secret of animal training is to 'give them a lot of love, trust and respect and they'll give you the world'.

I couldn't agree more.

See filmlivestock.com.au

Salt-water Man

KEVIN WARREN

'I STARTED FISHING AT THIRTEEN YEARS OF AGE;
I'M SEVENTY-NINE YEARS OLD NOW.'

So what's a bloke who has spent nearly sixty-six years as an ocean fisherman doing in a book about bushies? Well, I reckon he certainly qualifies. I decided that to be eligible you had to have worked and lived in or near a country town. Now, a town on the coast surrounded by mountains with a controversial but thriving woodchip mill testifies that there's timber around here. In fact, some of the most rugged bush country you will find is sometimes just a stone's throw from the coast. Eden on the southern coast of New South Wales is such a place.

Eden is a beautiful spot and has a great maritime museum called the Eden Killer Whale Museum, dedicated to the people of the sea and land. On display are many sea artifacts: old boats and all sorts of wonderful historical objects. Amongst the items are all sorts of whaling memorabilia, including the skeleton of

'Old Tom' the whale. Old Tom was famous for luring other whales into the bay, who were then killed by whalers. If you want to know about whales this is *the* place to come. Also on display is a timber-getters collection and history of the timber industry.

Outside the museum, and scattered around many sites in town are murals and mosaics that relate the whole history of the area. All brilliantly done by a former resident of Eden, the late Alexander McKenzie. I photographed them all and wandered streets looking for – and finding – more.

I asked many people who this Mr McKenzie was, but amazingly few people could tell me anything about him, and most didn't even know who had done all the artworks. Sometimes we take for granted what is in our own town. I went to the local cemetery and walked around. The groundskeeper there knew him and was full of other information about many of his 'clients'. It is a beautifully kept cemetery. According to the plaque on his grave, Alexander McKenzie was awarded an Order of Australia Medal in 1997, 'In the general division for services to the community and the arts as a painter and illustrator, particularly through the Eden Killer Whale Museum.' 'A busy useful life,' said it all. The plaque read – 32084 Warrant Officer II J.A.S. McKenzie OAM, Royal Australian Survey Corps, died 30 January 1998, aged eighty-six.

I finally tracked down his daughter and learnt more of him. I'll tell his story in another book.

But I needed to know about the live people I could interview in Eden; I knew what I wanted and was determined I was going to find it. I wanted a fisherman who had spent many years involved in the fishing industry. It didn't take me long to find one – numerous people told me about Kevin Warren. I would later learn that the Warren family has a long association with the sea and with this area. Kevin and his wife had just returned from holidays, and I interrupted him as he was unloading his gear. His handshake was firm and his face suggests a man with experience and one who has spent a life in the open. He is friendly and laid back.

We sat in Kevin's lounge-room as I took some notes. Outside it was sunny, but the wind was up and there were whitecaps on the bay. Kevin's home is just a few yards from Aslings Beach and looks across to the cemetery, where numerous Warrens, including both his parents and grandparents, rest in peace. You wouldn't expect old sea folk to reside anywhere else but close to the sea.

The first thing you learn when you take the time to talk with a man like Kevin is that the old ways of the sea are long gone. Here is a man who is now one of the old dogs of the sea. He is seventy-nine and has a lifetime's worth of maritime knowledge. He still lives for the sea, and he'll never really retire; he's just slowing down a bit with age. But he says he is lucky he is still pretty fit, with no major damage to his body from all that hard work of days gone by.

He is a man who started out his fishing life as a teenager, when all the boats had sails. It was a tough life. Nowadays it's all sonar equipment and GPS tracking systems. Now they spot fish from their own plane, and then guide their boat to where the action is, towards large schools of salmon, mackerel and such. Then they take their catch to their own family factory where it is frozen and packed. It's then shipped to the crayfish fishing industry in Victoria and Western Australia where their catch is used as bait and for eating. They even supply the bait industry on the Abrolhos Islands with container-loads of bait.

Before that, the canneries were paying 35 cents per kilo of fish. The bait industry pays $1.20 a kilo. Not hard to see why they gave the canneries away, especially once the one in Eden closed down and 300 people lost their jobs.

When the main timber industry shut down in Eden and the government paid out millions of dollars in compensation, there was a lot of money left over – some $12–15 million, apparently – they went around handing out money to assist the town. They gave the Warrens a $500 000 grant to help set up a factory of their own, to help employ people. Pelagic Fish Processors has been operating for about eighteen months and times are good. Now, up to thirty-five people work there on and off, especially when the tonnage of bait coming in is big. But fishing is still a challenge. Some days they come home with empty boats, while other days it is a big win. Kevin mentioned that recently they had 119 tonnes in one week, and sometimes they can do up to 300–400 tonnes a month. The factory is capable of freezing 100 tonnes a night. It can hold between 200 and 500 tonnes in freezers. It is an integrated business: factory, plane, boat. They now have the only licensed vessel large enough to purse seine for salmon in New South Wales. There are big risks – but big money is at stake.

'Probably the best thing was that we never fished for the money. When you are born and bred in the industry it's what you love to do, it's a challenge. We spot the fish from the plane and then go and try and catch them. We don't always win, sometimes they win, they win a lot, they get out of the nets and we come home empty. There's always the challenge. Don't get me wrong; it's nice when you have a big month, and a big cheque comes in. But there's bad months and even bad years. One in five is usually a very good year. The rest you survive,

you make a good living, but then there's the very good year, with big catches.

'We've upgraded our gear. Now we catch more than we used to in the last forty years. There're still large, even huge, schools of fish around. We bay fish, there's no deep sea, long-line trawling. The main reason we do well is that the predators of the deep are reduced in numbers – many of the predators have gone. I firmly believe I can't be contradicted by anyone. We're no longer allowed to fish north of Sydney up to the Queensland border. We aren't allowed to fish over the border in Victoria, or in Tasmania as we once did.

'We mainly fish for Australian salmon, mackerel, pilchards. We might go out and find twelve schools of 40–50 tonnes or up to 500 tonnes. Salmon are usually found just a couple hundreds yards off the beach. Salmon migrate from the Tasman and Victoria and up the New South Wales coast as far as about Port Macquarie, in what we call the Northern Run in winter. We get to fish both ways, because the water up north gets too warm for salmon, the Southern Run happens in summer. Some days we might fill the boat in a day. Sometimes it might take two or three. The boat can hold 60 tonnes of fish in refrigeration on board, and we could hold them on board for up to a fortnight.

'My son, Gary, runs the show now. He is a pilot; he runs the factory and he's teaching his sons. Grant, twenty-four, is the boat's skipper, and younger brother, Reece, twenty-one, dives for abalone. There are seven crew on board our boat, and we also have a second boat contractor from South Australia. Purse seine fishing isn't a consistent type of fishing. The boat does about 2000 hours of work a year. It's a 72-foot steel boat called *Janet I*. The boat is specially equipped: GPS, sonar, radar. The computer on board gives details of distance travelled as well as the water temperature. It usually runs at about 10 knots an hour in an eight-hour day. The average run would be between twelve and fifteen hours. We leave at night and usually arrive at the fish just on light in the morning. Ninety per cent of our fishing is done in daylight, sometimes at dusk or in the evening, but it's better to do it in day rather than under lights. I can say without fear of contradiction that it's better, we now get what the predators used to get.

'I started fishing at thirteen, been at it sixty-six years. I'm seventy-nine now. All of the hard work didn't knock me about much. Now though it's all hydraulics. We worked our guts out hand pulling in nets. If the winch broke, we did everything by hand. Now we have the very latest net hauler. Young fellas get it easy now. Our industry is good; we catch more than ever:

salmon, skipjack tuna, mackerel, pilchards, anchovies. We sell pilchards to Uncle Ben's of Wodonga for the pet food industry. We spot fish by aeroplane. We've had a Piper Cub, an Auster and now a Cessna 172 (with retractable undercarriage).'

And what does a bloke who has spent his life at sea do when he goes on holidays?

'We went fishing down the Murray. We go to Passage Camp, near Boundary Bend. Got some nice cod. We go there at least twice a year. It's old territory for the Warrens. My grandfather used to steam up the Murray to where the Murrumbidgee meets and then up the 'bidgee to Wagga. He died here aged eighty-three. I'm glad to be back from holidays. We are about to start a new big netting project. I'll design it and tell the crew how to build it; they do all the heavy work now.

'I still do a bit: I service the boat, I work with my grand-sons – they are great. I still do the odd trip out in the boat; I just like to be out there. It's a great thrill to put in a big net – it's still a real challenge. It's not a monotonous game. It's interesting, you might do two trips for nothing and then bring home 100 tonnes of fish. Purse seine fishing is very specialised. You can't just use a skipper off the wharf, no way.

'I'd hate to have to part with it – fishing. If I'd get the chance of a second go, I'd come back as a fisherman.'

The Warren family has been recognised for their long association with the sea. John Little's book, *Down to the Sea: The true saga of an Australian fishing dynasty*, tells the story of all the Warren families.

Robot-maker

TREVOR WALKER

'I DON'T KNOW MUCH ABOUT A LOT OF THINGS,
BUT I KNOW A LOT ABOUT NOTHING.'

There's no doubt he has had an interesting life and seen many ups and downs, but Trevor Walker has not let this stop him finding something to tickle the funnybones of other people. Everyone who sees his robots in action can't walk away without letting a smile go.

Trevor was born in Manchester, England, on Guy Fawkes Day in 1942. 'I was one of eight kids – five brothers and two sisters. I never knew my father; my mother brought us up and it was hard. I often saw her go hungry just so we could eat. I remember once when I was about eight I got caught by a local copper at the school after dark. The load of coke to keep the fires going in school rooms had been delivered, and I always took a bag there and pinched some for home. Anyway, a cop caught me one night. I got such a fright I peed my pants.

I told him I was taking it home as we had no heating and it was terribly cold. He said by the time he came back I'd better have filled the bag and be gone. We survived on donated dinners and got clothes once a year from the government. It was different in those days. Mum was stern and she used the strap if we were trouble, but only when we broke the rules. She once said that she didn't know how much the strap hurt us until it hit her by accident one day. But we deserved it, and I don't regret it, you have to have love and discipline, not just discipline, because it won't work on its own.

'My mum said Father had brainstorms, as he called them, and she said I was just like him, but actually it was bipolar disorder and I've had it all my life. We had fun when we were kids; we had no TV. A mate showed me how to make my first crystal set when I was eight, and later I built my own radio with valves and stuff. I always liked pulling stuff apart and electronics and such.

'At school I always got grade As for singing, metalwork and woodwork – the rest I wagged. The school was near a farm, and so with some mates I went chasing porcupines for their quills as souvenirs. I left school when I turned fifteen. My first job was as an assistant packer, but I eventually drifted into work as a trades assistant at an engineering firm, mainly heat and ventilation. I learnt to weld which was a great help for the rest of my working life.'

Being a bipolar sufferer means that life throws many high times and many low times at you. Not just normal ups and downs, but mood swings that are dramatic to say the least. When a down mood swing hits a person it is almost impossible to get through a day, let alone what may be weeks of debilitating depression. Trevor suffered to the degree that his bipolar swings worked on an almost regular three-month cycle.

'I changed jobs about every three months, and when down I'd just go and live with the street people, and then when up again I would go find another job. Often I ended up down on Torquay Beach and lived with other people who were called beatniks in those days, all bombed out. I survived by carving beach stones and selling them as sort of jewellery worn around the neck. I got 10 shillings each for them.'

Finally Trevor made a break for change in his life and emigrated to Australia in 1964. He flew out on Qantas. 'I started at Sandringham in Melbourne, then began work at an oil refinery doing welding, but three months or so later took off to Sydney and teamed up with an Aboriginal bloke who everyone knew as "Black Alan Barker". We lived in King's Cross and on the dope. Back to Melbourne and the refinery. That went on and off for years. Jobs were easy to get in those days. Later we hitch-hiked from Sydney to Perth across the Nullabor Plain. In those days it was just all bull-dust.

'In Perth we signed on with a circus, and on the first day we pulled ropes, fed elephants, moved bales of hay, and at the end of the day we reckoned it was the hardest we'd ever put in. We went out that night and when we returned in the morning the circus was gone,' Trevor laughs loudly. 'Then Black Alan left to go to Marble Bar in the north where he came from. I met up with Black Alan in Fremantle a few years back, he was in the street with his son playing didgeridoo and clapping sticks. They were making a few bob and then off to get on the piss. It was good to see him again.

'Anyway when he went to Marble Bar I went to Tasmania and was doing welding jobs, then I was flown to a job in New Zealand, welding in Auckland. Three months later I went walkabout around various spots in New Zealand before coming back to Australia. I ended up in Gladstone, Queensland where I worked at an aluminium plant.

'Soon after, I was living either in the bush or on Holloways Beach near Cairns. I first went to Cape Tribulation to live in 1968 and went back numerous times. It was the same over and over, work for three months and then go bush for three months. Someone once said to me, "Trevor, you are like a lavatory seat: always up and down."' Trevor laughs it off. 'It was later in life that I accepted this life of swings. About two years ago it seemed to change, and although I still get depressed, it's nothing like it was.'

Life for Trevor was a constant series of adventures in all sorts of places mixed with times of depression from his illness. But he had a way that made him get through, and he was always good with his hands.

When you talk to Trevor you soon find he has very little memory of dates or even years, but he often refers to things as happening 'when I was about forty-five', or 'when I would have been fifty-four' – that sort of thing. Sometimes his memory may seem disjointed, but other times he can sort out the years. Between 1976 and 1988 Trevor lived in Glen Innes, but he describes the time period this way: 'I arrived when I was thirty-four and left when I was forty-six.' Sometimes it is hard to work out what slots into where in his life, but Trevor was never a normal nine-to-five man, and life was always different to what some might describe as normal, whatever that is.

'At one stage I found an empty four-storey flour mill – an absolutely marvellous place. I talked to the centre manager and he asked what I wanted to do, and I replied that I wanted to start a restaurant and art gallery. He asked how I planned to

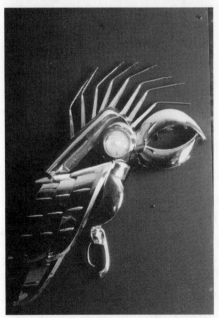

do it and I said "on the dole". He agreed to help and gave me $1000 worth of stuff from his hardware department, and then said he had a heap of ceiling materials, bits of this and that. He said he'd take a percentage of our earnings. So nineteen months later, with some friends helping, we even laid down a dance floor and a huge fireplace that you could walk into. We had been given some cedar panels and did the walls to make it like a real tavern. I'm no businessman, and when the money started to come in it all blew up and I had to pay out the others involved in it. The manager was a great guy but he got nothing in the end. I then bought one and a half acres and built a house out of an old house I'd bought and moved. Just after I got it finished it burnt down, just an accident really, so I left and went to Sydney.'

Using those ever-creative hands, Trevor began to make 'spider things' – clocks, bracelets and other jewellery with a spider theme. All were sold to shops in Sydney, and Trevor pocketed the cash.

When he was on one of his trips to Cape Tribulation in far north Queensland, Trevor had either lived in a tent or just in a sleeping bag on the beach. 'In those days, it was easy to just set up anywhere. I was at Old Forest near Kuranda at what was known as the Aboriginal Bakehouse, basically a big shed with shutters, a water tank and that was it. It was one of the happiest times of my life. We'd wash in the river on the flats, the Aborigines were nice people. People lived on the beach in the fifties and sixties and had veggie gardens in the bush. I made driftwood sculptures from wood I'd find on the beach or in the bush and made all sorts from fantastic shapes of timber; you just had to bring out the best in a piece of timber. Sometimes I did stone inlays. I sold them to the tourists and all you needed was enough to buy food, some polish, nothing much else.

'It was there I met the lady who would become the mother of our daughter. Our daughter, Catherine, now works in England in the British Council to do with arts and dancing. She's thirty-eight now, and has been involved in dancing all her life. She worked in many dance companies and has worked in England, Europe and America. She originally got her BA in Adelaide, majoring in jewellery and textiles. So I guess the creative things run in the family still,' he says with an easy laugh. He seems pretty proud of his daughter Catherine and rightly so.

'I was twenty-eight when I did my first chrome sculptures from car parts. In Melbourne back streets in those days I would often find abandoned cars or partly stripped ones, and I'd get the chrome bits, bonnet ornaments, etc. I never wrecked good cars, just abandoned ones. I collected tea chests full of all sorts of chrome bits from Holdens, Fords, Zephyrs and more. I first did big insects from bits, and then expanded. I'd sell them for an average of $80 to $100 – now they'd sell for thousands. I made probably 300 or more of them and people loved them. Later, when I was fifty-five, I had exhibitions of them in Paddington, Sydney and later at the Casino Reef Hotel in Cairns as well. I remember one bloke saying, "Now this is real art." I'd get a piece of chrome and sit down with the bits and move them around to try and work out what they are meant to be. When I know what I want, I then work out how to make them, how to screw them or put them together.'

There are no chrome sculptures left now, all have been sold and are out there being enjoyed by other people. All Trevor has now is some photographs of a few of them. It is satisfying to know that people are still enjoying them; they truly are works of art. 'Now cars are all plastic and there's nothing worth doing, like it was when they had the magic chrome pieces on them. The old cars had some amazing chrome.' How true. I have a number of chrome ornaments off old cars myself and they're now sought after and hard to get.

I'd come to this quiet caravan park in a tiny town to see Trevor's robots. I had first seen him briefly on a television program some years ago.

'I started to build my first robot when I was a kid of about eight or so out of a Meccano set, and when I moved here about five years ago I thought I'd better finish building one – it was my first robot. I wanted something to tax me, to make me think. A bloke said to me one day, "Where you going?" I said, "I'm going to the rubbish dump to make a robot." Three months later he saw the finished product and he just said, "You've done it! You're a genius!"

'I make robots from parts out of VCRs, printers, power supplies from computers, PVC piping, scrap metal, sound and light switches, fiberglass for moulding heads, optic fibres. I've got heaps of parts and stuff. I get most of the stuff from the rubbish tip and the $2 shops. Some electrics I buy. I can build one for about $350, but if you bought all the parts from Tandy or Dick Smith it would cost at least $1000 or more. I take things out of things mainly from the dump.

'One day I was putting on deodorant and the little rollerball in the tube gave me an idea for great eyeballs for my robot,' he laughs loudly. 'Some cheap kids' toys are great for bits, too. The $2 shops have all sorts of great stuff that you can pull apart and use some of the workings.'

The location of Trevor's abode has to remain a secret as he

no longer makes his robots and wishes to live a quiet life now. Others have heard of his work. Just recently a couple visited him who are trying to organise an arts grant to see if his creations can be put into a mobile trailer so they can tour around schools. He is keen to see the next generation take over and finish the rest of his collection. He now enjoys looking at the moon and stars with his telescope, and thinking of days past and dreams present.

'Robots are art for everyday people. Why? Because everyone just likes it. People don't feel like they've been left out.'

The Donkey Man

JIM WILLIAMS

'I ALWAYS DID THE ODD THINGS;
I'VE ALWAYS BEEN IMPULSIVE.'

Not many people can say they have had a beetle named after them, but Jim Williams can. He found a new species in the Bahamas in 1965 – a type of longhorn beetle – and it was named *Elaphidion williamsi*. I first met Jim when he was leading three donkeys through the back streets of a busy tourist town. The donkeys had advertising sandwich-boards on their sides. Jim was promoting an amateur theatrical show for a local charity. I took some photos and we chatted, and then I left him to it: the donkeys were keen to keep moving. I had his business card, but a number of years passed and I couldn't find him. I rang around and asking locals if he had moved to another town, but even then I couldn't locate him. I was determined to track him down. A lovely lady at a library knew of him and she made some phone calls and finally we caught up again.

I thought Jim was an Irishman, but turns out I was wrong. His father was born Vincenzo Di Guglielmo and had a pure Italian background, but was born in New York. He changed his name to James Williams. He worked as a sales manager for a large baking company. His wife and Jim's mother, Ethel had a German-Jewish background. She was a 'strong, strong lady who would make these feminists of today look like amateurs. She was tough and well ahead of her time.'

Young Jim has a brother John, who when he got married changed his name to Folk-Williams. 'He lives in California and is in professional mediation, working for the government of California. He's the white sheep of the family,' says Jim with a laugh. 'He's been quite successful.'

Jim is no slouch either. He was born in White Plains, New York in 1941, but grew up in Port Chester, New York, where Connecticut and Westchester meet. After he finished school, he went to the famed Cornell University and did a biology degree, with an emphasis on entomology. 'I was always interested in insects,' he says.

'After I finished university, I went to the Bahamas for about nine months, as Dad had ended up there and was running a restaurant-nightclub. That was where I met two Aussies. I'd been interested in Australia for a fair while; you know, I was young, and had a romantic dream of a land far away over the rainbow. I'd first met Aussies at university; a favourite lecturer had married an Aussie and I was always impressed with Aussies whenever I met them.'

Jim's wanderlust saw him take passage on a converted war-time liberty ship, an old freighter that crossed the Pacific and arrived in Brisbane on Currency Day – 14 February 1966. It was also Valentine's Day.

'I ended up working at the University of Queensland for a few months, studying some bug that wasn't very interesting – *Nysius vinitor*. I quit because I had a crazy idea I wanted to go cutting sugar cane, and ended up near Innisfail in 1966. The hand cutting of cane was finished and the machines had taken over, so I worked there for a while. I was working with an Assyrian and an Armenian and I was sort of their interpreter, but for some reason one of them ended up punching me to the ground twice, and when I got up for the third time he was coming at me with an axe, so I got out of there. I never really knew why it all happened.

'I went to Cairns for a few months before getting a job at Monash University in Melbourne for eight months as a lab assistant, a jack of all trades. Then I fell in love and moved back to Queensland, but it didn't work out; it was just a wild goose chase.

'In 1968 I saw an ad in the paper for teachers, and so I got a job with the Victorian Education Department. I absolutely loved it, and the students loved me, and for the next twenty years I taught biology, science and maths at high schools all over the place – Cheltenham, Castlemaine, Beaufort, Red Cliffs, Ballarat. I had married in 1971 and had a daughter, Magdalena. I married again in 1979, but again divorced in 1990. My biggest mistake – she was a damned good woman. Anyway, to cut a long story short, I ended up retiring due to a stress-related illness in 1988.

'In 1989 I did a librarians' course, and then spent the next few years renovating houses and getting involved in a number of organisations like Peace Link Ballarat and Gun Control Australia. I wrote a lot of articles for magazines and helped with campaigns. The gun control issue brought out a lot of emotions: I remember at a rally in Melbourne one bloke punched the brochures I was carrying out of my hands. I had previously belonged to gun clubs myself, so I wasn't ignorant of the facts. I wrote articles about ammunition control and other gun issues. I think we did a lot of good. I can understand why it was so emotional; men, I feel, have been stripped of a lot of their roles in society. It was a city against country thing, too. The gun debate brought it all to a head.'

In 1991 and 1992 Jim got involved with a local community radio project, before it was off to Byron Bay where he lived on and off up until 1996.

'I wrote a book that was published in 1997 called *Letters from Byron*, which was launched by Mungo McCallum and did pretty well. I worked at the Environment Centre in 1994 on koala issues, and had a major involvement in the setting up of the Writers Centre at Lismore in 1995. It was when I was at Lismore that I saw a photo in the paper of two people who had just come off the Great Dividing Trail with three donkeys. I knew nothing about donkeys, but joined a donkey society and ended up with two hopeless donkeys. But I learnt a lot.

'In 1996 I had sold a property at Armidale and was staying with friends at Bellingen, but it was so hot and humid that one day I thought I was going to kark it so it was time to go back to Victoria. I knew people near Daylesford, and I stayed with them before buying a few acres on the Great Dividing Range at Bullarto where I rebuilt the house over the next few years. By 1999 I knew a lot about donkeys and felt I was ready for a long walk. No one had taught me; I had to teach myself. The day before I left I had all my gear on the donkeys for the first time. By the end of the first day, the lead donkey had worked it out and was okay and settled into the task.

'My first big trip with Sancho and Platero the donkeys was in 1999, and it took us from Victoria and into New South Wales via every back road we could find. Since then the various trips have taken us to well over 3000 kilometres.'

The first trip that Jim and his donkeys did in 1999 covered quite a bit of territory – from Bullarto he took as many back roads as he could find, away from the busy traffic routes to the edge of Chewton, Sutton Grange, Axedale, Rochester, Shepparton, across the Murray River at Yarrawonga, Corowa, Wagga Wagga, Cootamundra, Wombat, Young. His many interesting encounters with people and places could fill a book, but at Young his adventures came to an abrupt end. He received word that his house had been broken into, so after six weeks of travel he loaded his donkeys onto a truck and hitched a ride back home.

It wasn't until 2000 that he set off on what he calls part one of the Y2K trip – Bullarto to Ballan, Inverleigh, Winchelsea, Otway Ranges to Forrest, Simpson, Timboon, Warrnambool, Heywood, Nelson, over the South Australian border to Mt Gambier, back to Casterton, the Grampians and again hitched a ride back home. He was worn out. All this was done walking – not riding his donkeys.

Before long, Jim had the wanderlust again and wanted to continue part two of his year 2000 trip. Leaving Bullarto, he went via the Murray River again into New South Wales, from Tocumwal to Berrigan, Urana, Lockhart, Wagga, Temora, Gulgong, Mudgee and again headed south to Harden. His donkeys were worn out and so was Jim after three months of walking, as well as packing and unpacking daily.

Jim's last big trip took him from home to Kyneton, Broadford, Flowerdale, Toolangi, and into the high country of the Bicentennial Horse Trail, past Marysville, Kevington, Jamieson, Snob's Creek, Alexandra, through the Strathbogie Ranges, Ruffy, Longwood, Nagambie, Greytown, Heathcote, Redesdale, Malmsbury, Drummond, and then back home.

'Days varied – from 12 to 32 kilometres. I always tried to be packed up and on the road by 9 a.m., ready for four hours of walking, and then after lunch and a break, we would walk for another four hours in the afternoon. The donkeys walk an average of 4–5 kilometres an hour, but it's constant; they never flagged, in fact often they dragged me up the hills and mountains. They were marvellous.'

On his return, things changed in Jim's life. He became involved in Rural Australians for Refugees and helped them advertise a play to raise money. 'I've always helped left-of-centre support issues.' In 2003 he sold his home and moved into Daylesford to live, as he had met and married a lady with a disabled child. 'I devoted my life to them and to helping them. I believe everyone should be treated decently.' Jim rebuilt much of the house there and did a lot of maintenance. Sadly after one emergency after another, Jim and his wife realised they weren't suited and eventually they separated.

For the last few years Jim has been writing articles for *The Edge* and letters to the editor about forest issues. People urge him to write the letters to newspapers and politicians on a variety of issues.

Jim is not a man to sit about: he always has something to keep him occupied. He is currently restoring an old wooden loom; he collects odds and ends from markets and does them up to look like new. He writes and performs his own poems at local cafés and various venues. His current passion is art, and when I arrive at his place hidden away in the forest he was painting his latest piece of art for a local charity exhibition. 'I don't regard myself as a great artist, but I do enjoy meeting other artists.'

When Jim had moved into town he had to sell his three donkeys. He still misses them, but has some new goals to achieve: 'To buy two new donkeys, to buy a new block of land and build a new home from scratch all by myself.'

Something tells me Jim will do it, and his wandering days with his best mates aren't over yet.

Timber & Tipis

DON O'CONNOR & SUE EWART
'MAY YOU WALK IN PEACE AND BEAUTY.'

As a lifelong collector of all sorts of antiques and 'old stuff', I thought I'd died and gone to heaven when I walked into Don O'Connor and Sue Ewart's factory. I have a collection of very old cogs, sprockets and wheels made from either wood or cast iron, all off some ancient machines from a century or so ago. Don and Sue's factory has an amazing collection of not only wheels, cogs and sprockets but the original machines which they are still attached to – the same machines they use daily in their business – the Timber Benders. As most of the seven main machines were built between 1850 and 1860 their factory almost overwhelms with nostalgia. I could live in the place – it has so much appeal for anyone who loves 'old stuff'.

Don O'Connor and his wife Sue Ewart ('We are married but I couldn't get used to who Sue O'Connor was,' says Sue) are the sort of people who are not afraid to 'have a go' and put actions behind their words and beliefs.

'We met via Don's last wife,' says Sue. 'We had similar beliefs, and we met in 1995 at an event where Don was conducting a sweat lodge and I was teaching drum making. We are from very different backgrounds: my dad was a permanent army officer and later a physiotherapist with an OBE for services to blind returned servicemen. I had three brothers and we lived in the city. All very normal. I became a home economics teacher with a food service diploma. I worked at RMIT in Melbourne, and later in a gourmet food shop. Then I went into stress management and became keen on eastern philosophies. I decided to travel and spent one and a half years overseas; I went everywhere from London to Kathmandu. Back home I lived in a flat in Elwood and wrote food service reports, doing surveys for geriatric hospitals.'

'I'm a bush bloke,' says Don. 'In Elwood I used to get lost when just two blocks away from the flat. I hate the city – I'm still bloody hopeless in it. I was always involved with land; trees have always been a passion. I was educated in Ag. Science at Longerenong Agricultural College, then went onto my dad's dairy farm near Mildura. Later I became a farm manager in north-eastern Victoria, but I realised I wasn't a good employee. I was born in 1951, and by the age of twenty-six I wanted to own land, so in order to get quick money I became a shearer and shore sheep on properties in the New South Wales and Victorian areas of Holbrook, Walwa and Jingellic. My third son, Avon, is a shearer too. Jason is a fitter and turner, Timothy heads a drilling crew, and Lowan is a truck driver.

'We've both travelled a lot,' continues Don. 'I was always keen to find out who the hell I am. I'm passionate about the "unity of the tribes" and my spiritual ancestry. I discovered meditation when I was a shearer.'

Sue says, 'We moved from Elwood to Healesville in 1996. A year later we bought a 40-acre bush block near Daylesford, which became known by the local Aboriginal name of *Dja William*, or earth nest. We started to build our own straw-bale house – a low cost place; everyone has the right to a roof over their head.'

Now they have a home with a teaching workspace under one roof along with other buildings. Not content with just building their own place, Don and Sue have taught many other people how to build, by conducting weekend workshops. So far they have conducted nearly sixty workshops, and at least forty houses have now been built as a result of their teaching. For many years Don also wrote articles for *Earth Garden* magazine.

Don's work is on a wider plain however. Since 1984 he has been building native tipis. 'I saw one at Glenlyon Confest one night and its fire inside just looked spectacular, so I learnt to sew and then made my own. I was looking for a way out of shearing by then. Anyway, it really did happen on a small scale. Since then I've made and sold about 300, and am now making about twenty a year. We've sold them to all sorts of people and for many reasons – for the sake of childhood memories or just a wish to have one, to have a spiritual place in the backyard, for fairy parties, school camps, a wilderness camp in the Adelaide hills, for weddings and barbecues. We've sold them to a herbalist, uni students, a shiatsu teacher, travellers, local builders – you name it, all sorts. One of our customers is at Appin Hall in Tasmania. Appin Hall is owned and run by Ronnie Burns (the singer and interior designer) and his wife Maggie, and they care for children and families in need. We even sold a 25-foot one to Inuits (Eskimos) in Alaska. Others have gone to New Zealand and all around Australia, including one at Longreach Backpackers' Hostel and one at the Eulo Store in Queensland.

'I like to create a house from basic materials. I've studied a lot about tipis. The native Americans believe they are held together by prayer and intention. Over the years I've done a lot of environmental shows – a sustainable living show, a solar show, as well as many fairs and festivals. We are great believers in renewable energy,' says Don.

'An amazing thing happened at the World Day of Peace at Pipestone, Minnesota. Here I was, an Australian teaching local Indians how to pitch a tipi. Everyone got to know me as the tipi man. It was one of the weirdest things. I've been to America many, many times and spent a lot of time with native tribes. Sue has travelled to America heaps too and to Alaska as well, and we love it. We do it on the cheap, but we have an absolutely wonderful time.'

'We travel on rice and roadkill,' says Sue with a laugh.

Tipis by Don O'Connor is a business that 'runs along in the background', like their straw-bale house building and teaching. The umbrella term for all their businesses is called Gentle Earth Walking. Another of their business activities is the Timber Benders. Don has had a passion for native timber and Sue 'is the sleuth of the family'. Sue wanted Don to make her a timber drum hoop by bending timber into a full circle. This project finally led them to Echuca to an old factory to collect a hoop. They were amazed at the business in this tiny grey block factory with dirt floors, full of spider-webs and under-used machinery.

They drove home with the thought that if the opportunity

ever came about they wanted it all, even if it was just to put the ancient machines on display somewhere. As things happened, in 2001 a huge building in Daylesford came up for rent, so they went back to Echuca to negotiate buying the machines and learn how to become timber benders. They did their sums and bought the business on vendor's terms. They leased a flat 100 yards from the factory. After more or less eight days training from the previous owners, Don the timber lover was left to learn as he went. The business had its origin in Launceston in 1888. It was moved to Mebourne in 1900, and by 1950 it was at Fairfield. Jack Flynn, a maker of bondwood caravans, bought into the business at that time, eventually moving it to Echuca in 1974. When Jack passed away in the nineties his son Nigel took over, and Don and Sue bought the business from him.

'In 2002 we moved the whole lot from Echuca to the premises in Daylesford: we had four semi loads, various utes and car-loads full, and even me with an endorsed licence driving a 10-tonne truck,' says Sue with a laugh. 'With some of the gear we brought down, we didn't even know what it was for, let alone how to use it. By January 2003 we were supplying their small list of clientele, but we were also trying to increase our profile.'

Since then, the Timber Benders have expanded their horizons, and they have made window heads, skirting boards for curved walls, curved handrails for the restoration of the Fitzroy Town Hall, rims for vintage cars and carriages, carriage shafts, hood bows, mudguards, fascia for railway buildings, and even curved chair backs. Other jobs have included creating a 12-metre long curved bench-seat for the food court in Collins Place Melbourne, a curved wall for the Corner Pub in Crown Casino, a jarrah bar in Sunshine, some curved timber work for

Northcote Town Hall and South Melbourne Council, a curved spotted-gum inset for a seat in a Sydney park, curved chair backs for the Sydney Opera House, varied timber work for a million-dollar house in Semaphore, Adelaide, and many other varied projects.

While Ballarat's tourist attraction Sovereign Hill has a small bending machine, they only do limited projects, but with his seven machines and a whole host of extra factory implements, Don believes they are the only factory in Australia of its kind. It is in good hands with Don and Sue and their beliefs: Don says a prayer of thanks over the timber each time as he lights the machine to generate steam.

'It is really stimulating for me spiritually working with the elements of water, wood and fire. I'm sure the timber talks to you; it's a very personal relationship – you, the wood, the machines. For me, I am just learning, always learning, and I am doing something that is useful for society. I'd love to employ apprentices and teach young people, but with today's Occupational Health and Safety laws they wouldn't allow it, due to the age and the way the machines are set up. They've already been here and checked the factory out, and I'm limited in some ways as to what I can do.'

So what was the history of these wonderful machines before Jack Flynn had them? The patent for the machines dates back to 1838 in the US, and the patent for the pressure unit dates back to 1843, but these are Swedish-made machines. In Melbourne in the early 1900s there were nine bending companies, but by the 1950s there was just the one left. Don believes his machines were built in about 1860, because they had been imported to Tasmania in 1888 and the shipping documents show then they were second-hand, thought to be about twenty years old.

The machine is capable of bending all sorts of timbers, and experience has taught Don to steam the timber for one hour for every one-inch thickness of the timber. The heating tubes, where the timber is steamed, can take timber up to 1-foot wide. Don's talent really comes to the fore when you watch him work. Getting the right curve on a long piece of timber means he needs to straighten it back out to an exact curve. After a few measurements and by drawing with chalk on the factory floor, Don soon had a perfect arch – curved to just the right dimensions. But don't think it is all that easy. Watching him work on a number of machines soon left me in no doubt that this was a man who not only knows what he is doing, but loves doing it with a passion.

Don bends all sorts of timber – American white ash, oak, beech, New Zealand white pine and elm. Native species include jarrah, karri, Victorian blackwood, redgum, Queensland silver ash, messmate, silver and black wattle, King Billy pine, sassafras and spotted gum. He thinks he can probably even bend ironbark.

What a craftsman! What a great bunch of wonderful machines!

A few days later I went to Sue and Don's property to take some photos. Sue took me around their property and talked of their love of the land that fills them with so much satisfaction. It is a lovely property, and Don was working on their home. They are always working and adding to the place with yet another project.

I wanted to know what was the interest that tipis held for Don and Sue. I knew it was a part of their spiritual life, but I'll let Sue tell it in her own words.

'The Lakota people of North America believe that their tipis are held together by prayer and intention, not just rope and sticks. When felling trees prayers are said and gifts given in exchange (generally ceremonial herbs to mother earth), and if a tree expresses the desire not to be part of a tipi we do not cut it. This is a feeling that you can pick up on when out working in the forest. When pitching, we walk four times in a sun-wise direction, walking the rope around the bundle of poles, prayers are said to the four directions and the totems, guides and energies of that direction are called into the tipi. The door of a traditional tipi is low to remind us as we bow to enter to say a prayer of gratitude for our shelter. The top of a tipi is opened and closed off from time to time, using the smoke flaps to direct the smoke and deflect any rain; however, some drops will enter the tipi and the native understanding is that this is a blessing, and they say a prayer of gratitude. The drops gener-ally fall behind the fire-place in the centre of the tipi, and this is where your altar is set up.

'The energy inside a tipi when all is put in place correctly is incredible – we liken it to the space in a chapel, or the energy of the pyramids. The restfulness and dreaming possible in a tipi is magnificent. Watching the fire inside your tipi while snuggled up in bed is also a wondrous experience, too, as is the view of the stars from your bed.

'The spelling of tipi came from the plains Indians them-selves – when they learnt English they chose "tipi", and not the French "tepee". We prefer the native spelling.

'We prefer not to add windows or zip fasteners to our tipis as we believe this is an unnecessary western addition to a truly exceptional design. Tipi poles are best when they are full sap-lings, rather than demountable poles. The native understanding is that the energy travels from mother earth to grandfather sky up the poles in a fluid, unbroken form. Metal poles are a no-go as they make great lightning conductors.

'Decorating a tipi is the prerogative of the owner, and it's recommended that this be in line with their original story or dreaming – if the owners sells the tipi, the artwork may be passed on with it, but the artwork is never repeated unless the tipi has been destroyed. Children love the energy of a traditionally pitched tipi, and we find that often we become a haven for them at fairs and public shows – the parents come looking and their children are happily playing in the tipi.'

You can buy a 10-foot tipi with no poles or lining for as low as $900, or a fully lined tipi up to 25 feet with twenty-three poles for $6800. If you prefer, you can camp in one of their tipis for $33 per person per night for a basic tipi, or up to $120 per couple per night for a luxury tipi.

Don and Sue share a real belief in what they do. Don says, 'If the people can tap into the real human spirit, nothing is impossible. Follow your beliefs. I work in the past, but I create value for today's generation. I like to create things. We like to create buildings that have a spiritual connection.'

And Don and Sue's big project for their next home is going to be something very different. Imagine a wooden Viking ship upside down, sitting on a base of stone and backed up to the side of a hill. Inside the 70-odd-foot long, 18-foot wide building, the roof will look like the ribs of an ancient ship. 'We've learnt a lot from other cultures and we want to attempt to recreate a spirit connection with our ancestors,' says Don. 'It will be a house just for the two of us. We want to live in the environment, with a back wall of stone and water passing down it and across the floor, past a fire-place and back outside.'

I told Don and Sue about my favourite architect Frank Lloyd

Wright, and the magic building he created called Fallingwater at Mill Run, Pennsylvania. He had a waterfall and a huge rock in the middle of a lounge-room. They need to read about it.

I like the sound of their Viking-ship house, and with their timber-bending machines; I can almost see the amazing interior of their dream home. 'We will make a feature of the timber ribs and the solidness of the boulders, and bring the water in to acknowledge that we want to be "in" the environment, not apart from it.'

Don and Sue are people who aren't afraid to be different to the 'norm'. Sue is the strength behind Don, as he is for her. They try to act as one of their brochures says – 'May you walk in peace and beauty.'

Mission in the Mountains

DAVID OLDFIELD

'PHOTOGRAPHY MAKES YOU LOOK AT THE WORLD — MAKES YOU SEE
THINGS YOU WOULDN'T SEE NORMALLY.'

The sign on the gate said 'Coobaroo', and I had gotten lost
looking for it down dusty tracks, but eventually I arrived to
find David Oldfield waiting for me. Finding a nice log cabin
set amongst old trees, old farm buildings and dry paddocks, I
was here to meet a man I first saw in a double-page spread in
the Melbourne *Herald Sun* showing his photos of mountain
huts. I wanted to meet this man and find out more about his
wonderful photos.

He has a mission in life – a passion – and he is very good
at what he does. David Oldfield is an enthusiast of black-and-
white photography, and he has combined this interest with his
love of the bush: he wanders the high country photographing
old cattlemen's huts, as well as the mountains in general. His
work recording the century-old huts has proved not only

a rewarding experience for him, but has documented an important part of our history.

Whilst many greenies don't approve of cattlemen in the high plains, they don't mind sleeping in the warmth of those huts built by cattlemen over generations. Governments have treated the mountain families with disdain, and what was once a much-loved tradition is now fast becoming a memory. It is a pity they don't harass motorbike riders and others who treat the mountains as a place to let off steam as much as they harass the mountain cattlemen. Rough motorbike tyres rip into the soft landscape more than cattle hoofs. But let's not delve too deep here into the pros and cons of the mountains and of the bureaucrats who are supposed to look after them.

David Oldfield has photographed some seventy remote huts and is still at it. There were some 250 huts in the area when I interviewed him, but time waits for no man and the ravages of fire swept across his beloved territory in January 2007, wiping out over one million hectares.

'The number of huts lost in the 2007 fires was surprisingly small,' said David later. 'We expected to see many more go in these fires. I've already applied to Parks Victoria to have Bluff Hut, Ritchie's Hut and Weston's Hut rebuilt. Last time it took them two years to make a decision. There were a couple of smaller ones lost in the Howqua region, and as well as the recreated Craig's Hut near Mt Stirling. We lost one refuge ski hut up there also.'

Amazingly, tourist authorities talked about spending $300000 to recreate Craig's Hut – used as a movie set for *The Man from Snowy River* – according to reports that came through even before the fires were out. It is a tourist attraction. It is a pity similar monies aren't spent on all the original and historically valuable huts throughout the mountains.

David Oldfield is a Yorkshireman, born in 1942. His father was a TV serviceman, and during the war had worked with radios and radars. A young David went to grammar school in Huddersfield. At the age of fifteen he sold an electric train set so he could buy a Kodak Sterling camera and 120 mm film, which gave him two-and-a-quarter by three-and-a-quarter inch prints. All black and white in the 1950s – no colour film available.

He joined the local Photographic Society as the club had their own darkroom. 'Oh the joys of the darkroom,' he recalled. 'The club taught me just about all I know about photography. On Sundays we used to go on club outings to the Lakes District, the docks and other places to photograph.

'Afterwards I went to university, joined Birmingham University Mountaineering Club (the Stoats), gained a lasting love of Snowdonia in all her moods and became a chemist. Then in 1967 I came to Australia and married Sue in 1975. We were both members of the Melbourne Bushwalkers Club, and with no children we were able to spend a lot of time in the bush. I used to have to convert my bathroom into a darkroom, but I still enjoyed photography.

'I ended up working as a chemist for the Defence Standards Laboratory in Maribyrnong for thirty-two years, working with plastics. In 1975 it became the Defence Science and Technology Organisation; the defence equivalent of CSIRO. I was in Research and Development. All overseas defence equipment that arrived in Australia had to be adapted to Australian conditions, and I was a part of making that happen. I finally retired to our farm in 1999.

'In 1980 we had bought part of an old property that was

being broken up into two blocks, so we bought 60 acres here on the outskirts of Melbourne in the north-west. In 1980 I started taking landscape photographs which were my main passion, and cattlemen's huts came later.'

As part of the bushwalking fraternity, David and Sue saw much of Victoria's high country; it was probably inevitable that David would start photographing the cattlemen's huts, even though he didn't know it at the time. The more he photographed the mountain scenery, the more he loved it.

'Huts were something I learnt to appreciate for their shelter from rough weather in the hills. They were just part of the environment, and gradually I felt I would like to take some photos of them, but somehow never got around to it, until in 1991 when I heard that Fitzgerald's Hut on the Bogong High Plains had been carelessly destroyed by fire, so I decided to embark on a project to make a photographic record of the huts before any more were lost.

'The huts are part of mountain heritage; they don't last forever, logs on the ground last about fifty years – we have to preserve what we have.

'The one thing I did with my photography was to shoot the huts from different directions and also to shoot the inside of the huts, which most people didn't back in the eighties.'

Wallace's Hut in the Bogong High Plains is a good example. David shot from the rear of the hut, whereas most people shoot it from the front, and the resulting photo is magic. It includes a beautiful gnarled gum tree in the foreground. That photo and many others were included in David's book *Havens of the High Country: Photographs from the Victorian Alps* published in 1996.

'Inside many of the huts are traces of all those who used

them years ago; they get richer as years go on, but texta pens are a pain now. The oldest graffiti I've found, however, was dated 1917. Overuse has become a priority; we were our own worst enemy. Few now who go into the bush even know how to light a fire properly.'

Sadly now the huts are the targets more often of mindless youth who see graffiti as part of life. Graffiti isn't art and it isn't a way to record history. 'Kylie loves Benjamin' scrawled within a heart shape on some rustic cut timber in a mountain hut just isn't right.

'March and November are the best times in the mountains. A good trip for me might be to photograph five huts, but a bad trip might mean I only get to one hut. I tried to get to the Charlie Mac Hut on three attempts – there's no easy way to it, and I found all the bad ways first – until I went way around and finally got there via a bush track down the Omeo road. The highest mountain hut is Cleve Cole Hut on Mt Bogong.'

David photographs differently to many other photographers, who nowadays use all sorts of equipment. 'I shoot only with the natural light that's available, even indoors. I use an aging 1960s Hasselblad camera that has been upgraded with bits over the years.

'Photography makes you look at the world – makes you see things you wouldn't see normally. My favourite photographer is the American Ansell Adams – my hero. I've got all his books. The way he uses light . . . there's just something about his work.'

David is a Fellow of the Royal Photographic Society and an Associate of the Australian Photographic Society of which he was president for two years. He is an exhibitor of mono-chrome prints on the Australian national circuit as well as a judge at camera clubs, at both national and international levels.

He gained a place in the 1990 and 1998 Hasselblad Masters Awards. Exhibitions of his photographs have been shown in the APS Convention Centre Hobart, Old Royal Mint Melbourne and Gippsland Art Gallery in Sale.

In 2003 fires spread across the mountains, destroying fifty-eight huts in the high country, and leaving over 250 that still needed to be cared for. The Victorian High Country Huts Association (VHCHA) was born as a result of this.

Historian Dianne Carroll and author Fiona Magnussen were two of the founders of the Association, keen to do whatever was necessary to keep the history of the mountain huts alive. David became its first secretary and still holds the position today. The whole of the mountain area from Warburton in the west to Corryong in the north to Genoa in the east is now broken up into areas by the VHCHA, and eleven areas each have a huts maintenance officer to coordinate efforts. The aim of the Association is to maintain and care for all huts, in conjunction with Parks Victoria and other public land managers.

Despite only operating since February 2003, their achievements so far have been noteworthy.

A replica of Horsehair Hut was built on a new site in April 2003, just a few months after the fires, to commemorate the loss of the original, which was the oldest high country hut in Victoria.

In January 2004 the Association held a Pioneer Skills Workshop in Omeo, which included the building of Roughriders Hut on the Omeo Rodeo Paddock. In April 2004 they rebuilt McNamara Hut, Buckety Plains on the original site and to the same design of the hut destroyed in the fires.

The Association's projects include: contributing to the designs of the new Federation and Mitchell huts; conducting major maintenance on Country Roads Board and Dinner Plain huts; cleaning up at Horsehair Hut; and looking after emergency repairs to Fry's Hut. New projects are tackled all the time.

Sadly it takes time for government departments to act. Once approval is given, volunteer workers get stuck into the task and rebuild huts quickly. Since cattlemen are now banned from the high country in most areas, the attitude by authorities is very much not in favour of the cattlemen. Many roads are now closed, tracks left to overgrow, bridges removed, areas locked off. While preserving areas for research and making sure that people do not have open slather on public land is important, nothing should be at the expense of people whose families have worked there for many generations.

'Real bushwalkers don't like greenies,' say David. 'We know the cattlemen and we work with them on preserving the huts. They are an important part of the heritage.

'The North-East Freemasons started work on the huts long before us, but they now are a part of our Association; there are many wonderful skills still being used on the huts. Skilled volunteers using traditional heritage techniques. One bloke, Graham Fall from Orbost, always turns up to hut projects, you should see him use a broad axe. He is a master craftsman. We have about 150 members of VHCHA, which is modelled on the Kosciusko Huts Association in New South Wales. We have about fifty members who are the hands-on workers. Anyone can become a member – either individuals or clubs.'

Echo from the Mountains, the Association's newsletter, is published four times a year. It keeps people up-to-date with what has been done, and future work parties, as well as other events.

They have also established a database of the huts to record details so that information won't be lost. David Oldfield has made a lasting contribution by photographing the mountains and the huts. In 2006 the Association produced a calendar using David's photographs. They also have produced a new one in 2007 using both his and other photographers' work. David Oldfield's photograph of a mountain hut appears in this book, and a publishing fee is being donated to the VHCHA.

I got to meet David and Sue's Italian sheep dog while at their farm. It is a guard dog for their many angora goats that Sue spends a lot of her time with. Due to the drought she was reducing stock on the day I was there and moving some on to new pastures. A final pat of their border collie and I was off; knowing that people like David Oldfield, with their passion and commitment, who will help the next generation see and learn about what mountain-life was like when people with fortitude and determination thrived.

This wonderful part of Australian history should not be neglected or forgotten, but treasured.

See also www.hutsvictoria.org.au

Stewie the Beekeeper

For a man who spent thirty-five years in high-risk construction industry work, Stewie now finds that being a beekeeper in the bush or working in his shed is more to his liking. He is a man who lives as he wants, and doesn't worry what other people think. He loves his bees and the quietness of the bush and life in a tiny country town. 'Just call me Stewie; no one needs to know the rest,' he says matter-of-factly, as he rolls another ciggie between fingers now attacked by arthritis. Those hands have been used in many situations, and what talented hands they are.

'I'll do a bit of bragging here,' he says, drawing a rough sketch of the Sydney Opera House on a piece of paper in his lounge room where we sit enjoying a beer. 'Right at the top of the minor hall of the Opera House,' he says as he draws the

199

familiar 'sails' of the building, 'I was the bloke who lowered the nine-and-a-half tonne flagstone into place as it was put there by crane. I also installed a lot of the steel-rib beams into place up there. I was a dogman standing on the block as it was being lowered and then I guided it into place and secured it. The crane was about a hundred feet above water and then I was on the steel cable high above the crane, so yeah, pretty high up – about 250 feet above the harbour.'

When I first asked Stewie about the Opera House he just breezed over it; he certainly isn't a bragger. In fact, I had to probe deep to get him to give me the full story, which gradually unfolded the more we yarned. From the dizzy heights working above the Sydney Opera House, Stewie also was often used to working hundreds of feet below water. 'The deepest I went was down to 370 feet below the surface, but that was in a pressurised diving bell. Often I worked 100 feet or so below in a rubber suit with an umbilical air hose back to the surface.'

Then he amazed me as he casually drew on his fag and said, 'I can't swim, but I can sink pretty good. In eight years doing underwater work overseas I did 936 dives on all sorts of jobs in various parts of the world.'

So how did he end up in a specialised construction and demolition job?

'I sort of fell into it at the right time, I guess. I ended up with all sorts of trade tickets – rigger, cranechaser, dogman, scaffolder, fork hoist, cranes, in fact I ended up after all the years with the biggest ticket in the industry, which covers just about anything you want to name. Anything that has to be lifted and moved I am licensed to do it. As a diver I was in the Professional Divers Association of Australia and in construction I was in the Federated Engine Drivers' and Firemen's Association as a rigger.'

Stewie is a staunch Labor man and a unionist. He was in the industry when times were tough and saw many fights to improve the conditions and safety of the men he worked with.

'When I first joined, you walked onto the job and hit a nail into a bit of timber to hang your coat; there were no toilets, or crib rooms to have lunch, no phones, few safety rules. All that came later after many hard fights and struggles with the employers. We often had to go out and just sit on the grass to get things done to improve conditions. They have it much easier now those young ones who've just entered the industry.

'I always wanted to fight hard to ensure we left the industry better than when we came into it for the next generation. I've seen times where the owners of the multi, multi-million dollar jobs would have a delay in arrival of goods from overseas so they'd make a case to stir up the workers so they'd go on strike, because then they didn't have to pay them while they waited for stuff to arrive. The bosses always had dirty tricks in the industry.'

The more Stewie and I talked, the more I knew that although I had come to interview a beekeeper about his work, there was indeed more to this quiet, unassuming man. So we go back to the start to learn more of this big, lanky man, who when he rolled a ciggie reminded me of Chips Rafferty.

'I was born in Rotorua, New Zealand, and my family had a dairy farm half way to Taupo. It was about 114 acres and we had forty dairy cattle and then Dad bought a second farm with about sixty dairy cows. We moved to Auckland eventually and us four kids went to boarding school. My sister Alison went to teachers' college and now she's retired. She is involved with my bees here; she's a great sister and still lives in New Zealand.

My brother Rick went through pharmacy training and is now a teacher in Perth. Another brother Colin was a great stockman – a sheep and cattle manager – but last we heard he was in Germany.'

Stewie first worked on the farm with sheep and dairy cattle before getting into the construction industry. He then worked building a paper mill in New Zealand and was one of ten who worked on the production line. He first came to Australia in 1962 to see the Commonwealth Games in Perth. He was billeted on a farm out of Perth as part of the Young Farmers Group. Afterwards he got a real taste for Australia by travelling with a mate to Adelaide, Melbourne and Sydney, making many side-trips to see the country. His mate went home to New Zealand to go to university, but Stewie stayed on in Melbourne and got into the construction industry there. In 1964 he drove around Australia in a Volkswagen, much of the time on rough, unsealed roads. For ten months he and a Canadian mate worked here and there as they explored Australia. They then went to Tasmania and did whatever work they could find. By that time Stewie was mainly working as a rigger on cranes and scaffolding and 'doing all sorts of horrible shit,' as he described it.

'In 1964 I ended up working in Broome, Western Australia working on the deep-water jetty, which was pretty amazing. The tide's rise and fall is 32 feet, so we worked with the tides, and installed the formwork for the concrete to be laid. I did a lot of that sort of work all over the place. In 1966 I worked on the Sydney Opera House, as I said before: that was one of the biggest jobs I've worked on. After that I went home to try and become a Kiwi again. I was on a multi-storey building job in Wellington, I'd seen the movie *They're a Weird Mob*, and it reminded me of my time in Australia. I thought, what the fuck am I doing here? So I saved a week's pay and was off back to Australia,' he says with a laugh.

'From about '68 I was involved for about seven years in the far north-west of Western Australia on a huge iron ore project in construction on screening and crushing plants. I did all sorts of jobs like ore handling, jetties, and I worked in places such as Tom Price, Port Hedland, Goldsworthy and Cape Lambert.

'In 1969 I worked on the concrete jetty at Port Hedland, which is 85-feet wide and can have two 102 000-tonne ships pull up beside it, it is shit-loads long. The rise and fall is 22 feet, and we would start work at 1 a.m. on low tide below the jetty, with huge arc lights. We'd strip all the form work out and crane it to the next section and install it ready to be built on with concrete later that day. We'd have to rush to get out before the tide rose above us, so we'd start to finish up about 4 or 5 a.m. and be finished work altogether by 6.30 a.m. Tides dictated all our work. I know we added 1200 feet to the length of the jetty. The huge conveyor belts would be loaded with iron ore that took it out to the ships for loading. Huge work.'

I wanted to know how Stewie got into diving and working on special underwater work.

'I sort of fell into it. In 1973 I was a rigging foreman in Eden, New South Wales on the dolphin-mooring system they were working on. I worked with two ex-abalone divers. I knew nothing about decompression or any of that. That was where I first dived. I had learnt most of my construction work and stuff at Altona in Melbourne, but I'd never dived before. But I soon learned, and was then qualified to be able to do other jobs.

'Between 1974 and '82 I did a lot of work on the Bass Strait oil and gas rigs. They found that many of the rigs when built weren't able to withstand the elements and so I worked as part of a support crew for English welding specialists, cleaning up and strengthening the welds underwater up to 180 feet below the surface. My job was to go down and build dry habitats for the welders to work in. Basically I'd go down the legs in full diving gear,' he says, as he again draws a mud map on the floor. A simple version of what he had to do follows.

'I'd go down and attach a sort of large box around the legs and a grill frame underneath for the welders to stand on. Then you'd release air from above into the box which blew water out and made a dry compartment full of air. My job was to construct and make sure it was safe to work in. Then the specialist welders would dive down and clean off all the old welds and re-weld and strengthen the leg. I did that sort of work on and off between '74 and '82 and would fly out in a helicopter, do the job and move on to the next.

'Do you remember when the ship Illawarra crashed into the bridge across the harbour near Hobart?' he asks. 'Yep, sure do,' I reply. 'Well, it ran into concrete pier nine, and piers eight and ten came down over the ship and sank it. There were 3000 tonnes and three sections of roadway on top of it. It sank to the bottom of the water – about 100 feet deep – and sat in nine feet of mud. When the engineers went to rebuild the bridge they found that the bow of the ship was too close to where they were going to rebuild the concrete piers. Tests found that the ship was moving in the mud. They had a monitor attached underneath. The ship was moving downstream by degrees, so I got a job out of it. As I said I can't swim, but I sink alright so I was attached to a line in full diving gear, wetsuit and full-face mask (called a Kirby Morgan). I had a communication line to the surface and air pumped in from above. I went down to the

bottom and I had to cut two feet off the bow of the ship to give some space. I worked with people from Maunsells, the original designers of the bridge. On display in the Maritime Museum in Hobart is a piece I cut. It is 8-inch thick steel and 5-feet long. You can imagine what it was like being 100 feet underwater cutting through 8-inch steel like that.'

'From there I spent five years in South-east Asia. I did diving jobs in Hong Kong Harbour, in the Philippines, Thailand, Indonesia, the Brunei oil fields and such. The overseas jobs were good, and made better money than Australia, but I learnt to spend it. On days off we'd jump on a plane and fly to some other country for a good time. I lived the life. I can speak a few languages pretty well: Kiwi, Australian, Thai, Malay. I can swear fluently in Italian, too. In fact, I reckon I can speak to anyone from the South Pole to the Chinese border because once you understand the basics of the old Greek roots of language and other stuff, you can recognise lots in different languages. I also chased a lot of women around then and even caught a couple.' By 1981 Stewie was back in Australia.

It's time for another can so Stewie leaves to get another one from the fridge. 'You've had an interesting life then,' I say out loud. 'Yeah,' he calls out as the fridge door slams shut. 'Yeah, why not? Better than being bored. Mind you, it has come with its problems. Getting bent a few times from deep water diving didn't impress me.' 'Getting bent' is divers' lingo for getting the bends – the fear of all divers – something that can kill.

'I was lucky I only got it three times, and it was just the pain bends in one joint,' he says as he rubs his arm. 'People get a lot worse and some die. It makes scar tissue under the skin and nitrogen bubbles come from the blood into the flesh, and the bubbles don't dissipate. I got the pain bends in my right arm three times. But you think, fuck you, I don't want it to take me. I was nearly killed when down at 370 feet in the diving bell; the idiot controlling the air on board didn't send the air mix down and I knew I was in trouble, so through the communication button that went back to the surface I was abusing the shit out of him. By then, though, I was talking in "duck"; you know when you get a helium balloon and let some of it into your mouth and you talk with that funny high-pitched sound. Well, I was abusing the shit out of him in duck talk, and he couldn't understand me at first. He was sending jack-shit air down the umbilical line and I was in trouble. So I say, "Get me up and outta here." So I was hoisted back to the surface. I was fuming. They weren't happy with me, but I wasn't going to die because the idiot didn't know what he was doing.'

As he settles back into his armchair, Stewie reflects more. 'Yeah, it was a pretty interesting time. I got to do a lot of travel paid for by companies and got paid as well. I chased a lot of ladies, and, as I said, I caught some, but as you can see I'm single and live like a single man. No kids. Not that I know of, anyway,' he says with a chuckle. 'I turn sixty-four in October 2007, and now I just enjoy working with my bees. I also repair all the local kids' bikes whenever they break down.' In Stewie's shed and yard, amongst his beehives, are bikes and bike bits and pieces everywhere. He is also very much into working with wood and has built his own huge 36-inch round sander. 'I can take an old or weathered bee box and sand it back in one action, rather than using a 4-inch job that takes ages.

'The reason why I took on repairing kids' bikes was so I'd have no problems with the kids. They don't throw stones on my roof or vandalise anything; they know if they did then they'd never get their bikes fixed ever again. They are all pretty good to me, and I have good neighbours – we all help each other.'

'So when did you give it all away, mate?' I ask.

'When that bastard Premier Jeff Kennett changed all the rules and I felt made my industry a harder place to work in. All those years of training and knowledge and what these hands could do and pass onto the next generation, I thought – after thirty-five years I can't be in this any longer. You can't help but become radicalised when you see what politicians and big companies can do and get away with. It felt like my industry was shot to pieces. I always had the thought that I was a custodian of the construction business, and that I should leave it in a better condition than when I entered the industry, but well, I saw so much and decided I didn't want to be a part of it any longer. I had contract work over the years and I might not have been the biggest employer, but I did care about what I did.

'I retired in October 1994 and got into beekeeping the same year, but I picked tomatoes during the season for a while. Now I'm a hobbyist beekeeper with thirty-odd hives, and I keep my friends in honey. I love it, I wish I'd known about beekeeping forty years ago; it is a great lifestyle and if I had, I'd be driving a Mercedes by now. But I love the ute and my sister, who happens to be allergic to bees, is keen for me to keep doing it.'

It was time for me to hit the road, and as I left, Stewie handed me two jars of his honey – one white gum, one grey box, which is on a piece of toast I am having with a cuppa tea as I write this story. Good stuff, Stewie; I'll be back. When I asked if he had email, his reply said it all about the man who loves to tinker in his shed and go chasing bees in the bush. 'Nah, mate, it is my ambition to end up looking out the hole before they close the lid and bury me, knowing that I never turned a computer on.'

And his final word for the next generation: 'Don't do anything you don't like. When you find what you like, then really get full on.'

Boomerang Woman

LEANNE LOVELAND

'I'D LIKE TO SEE A LOT MORE KIDS THROWING BOOMERANGS –
THEY GET SO MUCH FROM THEM.'

Leanne Loveland is Australia's only female boomerang manufacturer – and she's a champion boomerang thrower, too.

Her father Bernard 'Bunny' Read was 'always good with
his hands' and 'a big kid at heart'. Curiosity was the reason he
made his first boomerang in the 1960s 'just to see if he could
do it'. He bought his first boomerang at the age of ten. It took
him a little while to get it to fly, but he'd gotten the hang
of it by the time he was a teenager. What he wouldn't have
imagined at the time was just where his curiosity would lead
him. He ended up in the *Guinness Book of World Records*,
became a four-time world champion, built a business, travelled the world, and even after his death his family is still
throwing boomerangs. Not a bad epitaph for a country train
driver. He was also a good footballer and golfer. His 'hole in

one' is proudly commemorated on a wall of the Wycheproof Golf Club.

The boomerang is an Australian icon, and was developed centuries ago; the non-returning variety was once a valuable hunting tool among many tribes around the world. When used properly the boomerang can be a very deadly weapon used for gathering food. I like one English dictionary's description that it's 'a bent or curved piece of hard wood used as a missile by the native Australians, one form which can be thrown as to return to the thrower'. Get one behind the ear and you'll testify to its use as an effective piece of weaponry. Bunny called the boomerang the 'thinking man's frisbee'. He could even get a boomerang to do a figure eight.

Bunny Read died in 1994 and now his Wycheproof Boomerangs business has been reinvigorated by his daughter Leanne, who won her first boomerang throwing competition at thirteen to become Junior Australian Champion. She was also Victorian Ladies Champion. Her son Ben won his first under-sixteens competition for throwing accuracy when he was just twenty-two months old – the youngest sporting champion in Australia! 'Baby Ben' Loveland made the front pages of newspapers across Australia and America, including *The Washington Post*, and has had many newspaper articles devoted to him over the years. He was three feet tall when he became a champion. Now many years later he is happy to quietly make boomerangs part time for Leanne.

Even the next generation is getting involved: Leanne's four-year-old grandson Isaiah is already a super boomerang thrower. Bunny would be a proud man.

Bunny was a train driver in South Australia, and Leanne and her sister Debbie were born in Bordertown but lived at Serviceton until the family packed up and moved to Wycheproof in country Victoria in 1967. Wycheproof is famous for two things – the railway that passes down the main street of town, and Mt Wycheproof, which at 43 metres high is one of the smallest mountains in the world. It's also where the 'King of the Mountain' competition is held: entrants have to carry a bag of wheat to the top of the mountain. Wycheproof should also be famous for inspiring the man who became the World Champion Boomerang thrower, but sadly there is no mention of him anywhere. A statue of Bunny throwing a boomerang would be a fitting tribute to the man and a tourist attraction of a different kind – probably the only one of its kind in the world. C'mon Wycheproof! I am going to make sure the Shire President reads this story. After all, since Bunny Read started making boomerangs in Wycheproof in the 1970s, there have been four generations of his family who have become expert boomerang throwers. Not a bad effort, I reckon.

The two Read sisters were going to school in 'Wychie' when Bunny's interest in boomerangs grew. It was 1975 and as he sat in his car at Swan Hill watching other boomerang-throwing competitors, Bunny thought they were too good and that he wouldn't be able to compete. But he had a go; he had a good throwing arm and he came third. From then on he was hooked, and soon his hobby became a way of life. The family became involved: his wife Heather always supported her man, and even helped by cutting out boomerangs on a band saw for him. She also sat in the sun on many occasions watching Bunny compete, just to be there as his supporter. She will still help out in the factory if required. Bunny went on to hold an Australian record of 112 straight catches of returning boomerangs. He later increased that to 146 consecutive throws.

That record has now been beaten. In 1974 he topped the field in three separate specialised competitions held at Melbourne's Moomba Festival. He also won events such as the shortest time for ten catches; most accurate return, and many, many other titles over the years: Bunny won the World Championships in 1975, 1977, 1978 and 1979. He won the Albury Championships in 1979 and 1982, the South Australian Championships in 1982, the Australian Championships in 1982 and the Victorian Championships in 1983. He was nominated for Sportsman of the Year in '82/'83 by the Sports Federation of Victoria. He was also runner up in the Australian Championships in 1983, 1985, 1987 and 1988. His world records also included consecutive catching, fast catching and largest returning boomerang. He once described successful boomerang throwing: 'accuracy and distance play a major part, but you also need plenty of speed'.

Many of Bunny Read's achievements were filmed for television programs such as *You Asked for It*, *Ask the Leyland Brothers*, *That's Incredible* and many overseas programs, including being interviewed by David Frost for the BBC. He was the subject of a special documentary made by the Australian Information Service, which was sent to embassies throughout the world to promote Australia.

Bunny opened the Wycheproof Boomerangs factory in a shed in the main street of town. It was after coming third in a competition using a 19-inch conventional boomerang that he decided he needed to make his own and was inquisitive as to whether he could make them go further. His first boomerang was made from marine ply, shaped by hand using a wood rasp. Special machines would come much later.

When he won comps people would ask him if they could buy a boomerang, so he started making them for people in

1973, and began selling them while he was still working on the railways. He sold locally, but as his name grew he was approached by Richard Harrison of Louisiana, US, known as the 'Boomerang Man'. Bunny expanded his business and sold them to Richard. Leanne still sells boomerangs to him.

In his day Bunny built up a good market for his product, not only in the US but also in England, Germany, Holland and France. His name was synonymous with boomerangs. At one stage he was making 25 000 boomerangs a year. Once he was asked to supply 100 000 boomerangs to Peru, but he decided he couldn't meet the order as he liked to look after regular customers around the world.

Leanne showed me the many scrapbooks and countless newspaper articles about her father. He and Heather went on sponsored tours overseas to represent Australia and his travels took him to the US three times, to the World Design Expo in Japan, and to New Zealand for various World Cups. He did many promotional tours to Hobart, Launceston and many other parts of Australia. He certainly could be called Australia's 'Mr Boomerang'. No one promoted the boomerang better. He even showed his skills at a Scottish Highland Gathering amongst the bagpipes and in Jakarta, Indonesia. Bunny, Leanne and grandson Ben flew boomerangs on Boeing Field, at the Museum of Flight in Seattle, as part of a five week tour of the United States.

'Dad had many lovely friends in local indigenous communities, especially his good mate Hilton Walsh of Swan Hill.' Leanne is good friends with Murrundindi, an elder of the Wurundjeri tribe, and an ancestor of his signed the 1835 Treaty of Melbourne with John Batman. Murrundindi now works at Healesville Sanctuary doing story-telling, didgeridoo playing and boomerang throwing.

Finally, time caught up with Bunny, and he became very sick, so in 1990 he gave most of it away – he still made boomerangs but there were no more competitions. When he died *The Australian* newspaper devoted half a page to his obituary, and the *Herald Sun* and other papers carried tributes too.

In the end he believed the dodgy imported boomerangs that started appearing on the market in the 1990s were ruining the sport. The imported rubbish was made for the tourist industry and most would not return when thrown. They gave the industry a bad image – one Leanne is still working to overcome. Every boomerang she makes is a real one that comes back when thrown, and she spends a lot of time making sure the people who buy them are happy and know how to use them.

'After Dad died I lost interest and his machines were put away,' says Leanne. 'However, once I got the machines out again it was just like going home – it just felt right. I started it all again in 1999; first I was just going to fiddle with it a bit but soon I got into it and thought that maybe there's still a market. It didn't take long before I wanted to really do something with it. I knew nothing about business so I did a couple of business courses and I contacted all of Dad's markets again to re-establish it. Schools became interested and initially I spent one day a week at Pyramid Hill School with grade six students, showing them how to make and throw boomerangs. One special girl was really great; she had a good throwing arm and she kept in touch. She got blanks and then made her own boomerangs.'

Leanne loves kids and doing school trips, teaching and seeing the faces of kids when they catch their boomerang for the first time. When she decided to re-start the business she was making boomerangs in a small car shed, suffering from the

dust inhalation as she went. Her family has grown up, but all are still involved in the business and will pitch in when necessary. Sons Jeremy and Ben are good: Ben is 'very particular' and, like her father, great with crowds and demonstrating the sport. Jeremy is very good at making the boomerangs. Leanne's two daughters help in extra busy times. Sharna is a hairdresser and Kirby has her own makeup business. Ben is a baker. Jeremy is her main man in the factory. When she started the business in earnest she didn't know how to paint the boomerangs, but watching film footage of Bunny at work taught her to do special designs with ease and speed.

A new specially built factory and showroom was built in early 2006 in Junortoun Bendigo. On display is a large collection of boomerangs of all sorts, including the one her father made and used to get himself into the *Guinness Book of World Records* – the world's largest returning boomerang, which is a huge 71 inches.

The new business has been growing steadily since 1999 and now makes over 10 000 boomerangs a year and exports them overseas, as well as supplying them to all parts of Australia. Leanne markets to schools, operates factory/showroom tours, runs an advisory service to owners, and her website has been a boon, especially for overseas clients. Leanne taught a man over the Internet how to get the best from a boomerang, and he is coming to Australia this year to have one-on-one lessons with her. In the Netherlands a man bought one of the boomerangs made by Bunny at auction and is now in contact with Leanne.

Leanne is a busy woman with 'not enough hours in the day'. All the boomerangs made in the factory are not only handmade, but they're also flight-tested to make sure they are the very best quality. She also either hand-paints or silk screens them before packaging them with throwing instructions and posting them off to many parts of the world.

'I'd like to see a lot more kids throwing boomerangs – they get so much from them. My ultimate goal for the future is to be the absolute best boomerang company, and to overcome the dodgy non-returning tourist junk boomerangs. I can fix non-returning ones for people, and I love to teach the art of throwing. I'm not into competition throwing now, but I go to comps to meet people; I enjoy the friendship of the sport. There aren't as many comps now, but they're still going at Albury, Perth, Melbourne and Bairnsdale. New South Wales has a good following. The World Cup is in Australia in 2010 in Perth so I'll be involved with that. For me though, education is the priority.'

For all you people who love to win and would like to get yourself into the record books, here is a challenge. There is only one boomerang world record held by an Australian now – the hunting stick category – and that's with a non-returnable boomerang. C'mon, Aussies, c'mon – surely someone out there will rise to meet the challenge and reclaim some pride for the Aussie boomerang. The sport is big in the US, Japan and Europe, but it is Switzerland that holds the most world records in the 'Aussie Round' – a sort of Iron Man competition of boomerang hurling, distance, endurance, consecutive catching and trick catching. And would you believe that France – oh heaven forbid! – holds the juggling and maximum time aloft titles, while the US holds the fast catching title. It is time for Aussies to resurrect the sport and take on the world. Do it for Bunny Read and Leanne Loveland, who have given so much to the sport.

Leanne welcomes people to her new complex at Bendigo, where she will show you her boomerang collection; you can also see how they are made in the factory, decorate your own on the spot and then be shown by Leanne how to throw it and catch it on its return. School workshops and group bookings are welcome any time and can be arranged by contacting Leanne.

One thing is for sure, and that is that you will be shown the art of boomerangs by a passionate lady who grew up with them. I'm sure she will only be too happy to tell you all about 'Mr Boomerang' – Australia's master craftsman and king of the boomerang.

See www.boomerangsales.com

At Home with History

PETER SQUIRES

'I'VE SPENT OVER A MILLION DOLLARS ON THE PROJECT SO FAR, AND ABOUT TWO MILLION'S WORTH OF ELBOW GREASE AS WELL.'

Let me tell you, I'm the sort of bloke that could live in any one of Peter Squires' houses. All up he owns 106 buildings sitting in thirteen streets: houses, shops and much more. Peter's places date from 1860 to 1960, and I love them – original places from our bush history, not ones recreated to look like something from the days of old, but actual buildings he has saved from demolition or desertion. He moved them all to his own property and then did them up for display. No, you can't move in; they are all on display for tourists, and you might find it somewhat intrusive.

Mind you, it is an interesting walk around Peter's place. How many people can say they own a working picture theatre, a couple of butchers and bakers shops, a garage, fire station, church, cemetery, powerhouse, Cobb & Co offices, dentists, chemists, and even a house made of cow dung, plus a whole heap more buildings? Peter also owns about thirty cars, forty tractors, 150 engines, 200 old farm and agricultural implements, twenty-five horse-drawn vehicles, a riding horse, two clydesdale horses, two dogs, some goats and twenty guinea pigs. Add to that impressive list a huge collection of everyday items kept in almost every building he owns, and one can say Peter Squires certainly lives up to the title of 'collector'. He also has seventeen railway train carriages, including two full of extra items still to go on display. Oh yeah – and he owns 12 000 old records.

'I've spent over a million dollars on the project so far, and about two million's worth of elbow grease as well,' says Peter. 'I think the thing that amazes me the most, though, is how the trees have grown – ten-year-old trees now standing at up to 50 feet high.'

So how did this man get the idea to build his own town?

'Well, in 1971 I went to Swan Hill Pioneer Settlement in Victoria. I was so impressed with the idea of a pioneer village that I thought South Australia could do with something like it to preserve the state's history. I thought, if I don't do it, no one else will.

'Committees, I believe, are a heap of arms and legs and no brains. My biggest advantage is being able to make a decision and do it, to give the immediate authority to go ahead. I'm a great believer in paddling your own canoe, as no one else will do it for you.

'How it all happened was that my wife left me, and I thought: Here I am all alone with my son. I wanted to attract a new bird into my life, and I wanted a chance to meet a broad section of people, and if they'd pay to meet me, then all the better. Also I wanted to create something for the South Australian community.' Peter explains that he was talking to his mate Jock over a bottle of beer, and mentioned he might like to build a pioneer village.

'You can have the Peake Railway Station for $100,' says his mate, who was in charge of railways.

'I'll think about it,' says Peter.

About a month later his mate rang up and asked what he was going to do about the building. Frustrated by Peter's hesitation, he said, 'C'mon, you old bastard. Give us $100 and get on with it.'

So Peter did, and he got a local crane operator to collect it and drop it on site.

'Immediately, the State Planning Authority and local council were up in arms, demanding to know what I was doing. "You can't do it," they said. I said, "It's on freehold land, and I can do what I want."

'I was told to put it on paper – with eight copies of plans! The State Planning Authority would go up three weeks later to survey the site and consider it for approval. And that was the start of it – three years of negative negotiations.'

It wasn't until Peter got Peter Lewis, the local MP for Murray, in his office that things happened.

'He suggested we ring the State Planning Authority halfway through their monthly meeting and demand a vote on the application there and then. After ten minutes of deliberation, a reply came back that a majority of 6 out of 11 voted to proceed. Peter Lewis put down the phone and said, "You've got yourself a pioneer village – go for it."

'As far as I know the local council, the health department and the E&WS (Engineering and Water Supply Department) were all for it, but the ones who were against it were the high-ways department (because I was asking for public access off a 110 kph road) and the tourism department (because it wasn't a tourist-accredited area).'

So after three years of effort and determination, all that was left was to complete the project.

'I built up an association with Webb House Removers from Bordertown, and working with them, began to move old houses from all over the district on to my land. All the buildings have come from a 200-mile radius from places like Adelaide, Murray Bridge, Langhorne Creek, Finniss, Lameroo, Bordertown, Lillimur South, Francis, Hynam, Serviceton, Tailem Bend, Lobethal, Ashfield, Peake, Kalangadoo, Monarto South and Wolseley. I even bought the entire Hackham Pioneering Village, consisting of nine buildings, in 1992.

'The local people were very sceptical of my actions. Most people expected to see the project fold up, but my plan was not to go into debt and to have my motor business sustain the project until it created its own income.

'Criticism ceased and Old Tailem Town grew into a sustainable project. I only opened it on Saturdays and Sundays between April 1986 and January 1998, and then went full-time after that. We put through about 10000 people a year. Sovereign Hill puts through about 90000, but they have a larger population and huge amounts of funding through government tourist dollars, as well as a lot of free advertising. This is a private enterprise, and I must say it is harder to promote the project than to build it. I spend at least $25000 a year on promotions. About 60 per cent of people who go through are return visitors and people who have heard about the place from their friends and family.

'The tourism department is government run – they don't

come here to consult us or seek the kind of advice that we could give them being the people in the frontline of tourism. I wish they would have a different attitude to it all. They didn't see this as a tourist area in the early days and it hasn't changed much; they promote the Barossa Valley and places like that.

'All the buildings are real buildings with their own histories – that's the real reason why it is a sensation. These buildings breathe life into previous generations. The biggest thing is that we aren't pristine like Sovereign, not painted up like we're new; we are totally authentic. Sovereign Hill is really good, but we are different.'

'The picture theatre is fully operational, with carbon arc projectors from 1942. I badly need more 35 millimetre films and newsreels, though. Our hospital here is fully equipped, exactly as it would have been in the 1950s, with X-ray machines, surgical equipment – everything right down to the scalpels. There's even an 1850s operating table, a surgery, two wards and an operating theatre. These aren't just empty buildings or facades, these are the real thing.

'I paid cash for 70 per cent of all the artifacts here, and 30 per cent have been donated over the years. I removed the cemetery from a town with their blessing, as it was being vandalised – just the headstones though, not the underground contents.'

Another interesting collection that makes its home here is the Shepherd Display, run by Dawn Shepherd. Her late husband John and her family have always been avid collectors. There is a very large shed chock-a-block full of old restored stationary engines as well as many other items, such as a huge collection of tins like Arnott's biscuit tins, oil and grease tins, cigarette tins, as well as outboard motors, chainsaws, spark plugs, padlocks and keys, dog-tags, camp ovens, mincers, cameras, cigarette lighters, blow lamps, stoves, radios, electric jugs, medicinal household items and sewing machines. Also there are thirteen show-cases full of all sorts of interesting bits and pieces.

'The movie *Chuck Finn* was made here, and we've featured on TV seventeen times – on shows like *The Great Outdoors, This Day Tonight,* and *A Current Affair.* Over the years we've had many media personalities and well known people pass through: US actors Susan Day and Harry Hamlin made the American film *Disappearance* here; Australian actors Lynda Stoner and Ernie Dingo, tennis ace Max Willander, and politicians like South Australian Premier Lyn Arnold have all visited here. Bronwyn Bishop opened the picture theatre.

'I'm now sixty-seven years old and I still enjoy running the village, but I'm determined now to have three weeks' holiday sailing my yacht down the Corrong. It's a lovely 25-foot south coaster called *High Roller.* As well as that I'd like to visit my friends around Australia and overseas who I met through the village.'

Peter says his intention is to hopefully have his son take over the reins of the business after his own seventieth birthday, and after that he will play a backseat role. 'I'd love it to be here in thirty years, but fate will decide that.'

Peter has a long connection with this land. 'My grandfather was George Jaench, who worked on the old telegraph station. He was in charge of the Katherine Telegraph Station in the Northern Territory from 1900 to 1910, but he developed arthritis and couldn't work the morse code. My grandfather, along with Pat Gurrey and Thomas Row, was commissioned by the government to explore the Katherine and Daly Rivers in the Northern Territory in 1908 and was one of the first white fellas to go down them. Anyway, his father, my great-grandfather, owned 50 000 acres in this district and he talked George into coming home, and gave him 10 000 acres for him to farm. That land was here, and in 1923 he established Carranya Homestead. He died here in 1958 and my grandmother Irene died here in 1974, aged eighty-six. They both knew most of the characters mentioned in the book *We of the Never Never* by Aeneas Gunn from their time in the Northern Territory.

'The land was auctioned off in sections in 1976 and I bought the homestead block of 210 acres with a three-quarter mile frontage on the Murray River. I now live in the old Carranya homestead, next door to Old Tailem Town.'

Well, we know all about his creation – Old Tailem Town – but I wanted to know more of the man.

'Well, I was born in Adelaide, the only child of Lloyd and Nada. Dad was a car dealer and ran a panel beating shop right in the city. My parents got divorced and Mum remarried a Tailem Bend mechanic. I went to school in Tailem Bend until I was fifteen, then I did my apprenticeship with my step-dad. In 1967 I worked for his Chrysler Agency, Heynen Motors, for two years, before I went overseas to New Zealand and then Johannesburg, South Africa, where I made a fortune of £11 000 selling Chryslers. After that, I went to England and worked in Berkeley Square Garages for two years before buying a 32-foot trimaran yacht, and in 1969 with two mates I sailed from the United Kingdom to the Mediterranean, the Suez Canal, the Red Sea, the east coast of Africa and to Durban in 128 days. We had left England just a week before Sir Francis Chichester, when he went on his epic round-world trip. We met him a few times, but we were beneath him: he was a bit of a high-class snob.

'I sold my yacht *Nimble Days* in Durban, Africa when I turned twenty-five years old. I had given my word that I'd come home; I came home in 1971 and helped grow the Chamberlain Tractor Agency here to the biggest of its kind. We had 70 per cent of the Australian market. We also had John Deere as well. I ran Heynen Motors from when my step-dad died in 1986 until 1993 when I shut it down. I had been building here and from then on I worked here full-time, and Old Tailem has been paying for itself ever since.'

But what was the real catalyst for building Old Tailem Town?

'Well, I first married in 1968, and Daniel, my son, was born. He's now thirty-seven and has a wife, Bettina, and two sons, Tom and Scott. He's currently a mechanic. But my wife left in 1979, and I was all alone with my son, and I thought, "I need to meet people." In 1987 Margaret Clark arrived for a visit and she's been with me ever since. She doesn't get too involved here though; she's happy doing home duties next door.'

And what is the simple reason a man devoted his money and energy to creating such a place?

'In my opinion, the preservation of our heritage is one of the most important things in binding the future stability of generations to come. It's been a mammoth journey, but it's been a very satisfying time achieving this existence and a wonderful opportunity to see the results of efforts over the last twenty-two years in one place.'

With that, it was time for me to give Chuck the dog a last pat, shake hands with Peter and head off west, after enjoying a few hours seeing this dedicated man's wonderful achievement.

He has really 'paddled his canoe his own way'.

The Chook Lady

KRISTINA BROWNING

'ONE CHOOK JUMPED UP ONTO THE TABLE NEXT TO ME, UP CLOSE
AND PERSONAL – IT WAS A GREAT OPPORTUNITY TO DRAW HER FEET.'

Chooks?

Chooks!

Chooks have been good to Kristina Browning – both artisti-
cally and financially. She is well known for her art featuring
the humble chook. But don't think for a minute her work
might not be wide-ranging. Chooks may have helped her
create her alter ego, but her work is broader: she really is a very
talented artist. Coloured pencils, oils, printmaking and sculptures are all part of her repertoire. Still life, Japanese-inspired
printmaking – all sorts of subjects other than chooks are part
of this serious artist's world.

'I love chooks – we always had them when I was a kid. I've
got four chooks now. As kids we fed chooks pollen mixed with
water, and I was always eating it, too. When I was aged four,

Mum started working as a weaver at the Castlemaine Woolen Mill, and I was looked after by a family friend, Mrs Archer, who I adored. She and I would collect the eggs which had been laid by the dozens of chooks she owned. The eggs were everywhere around the property and along the creek banks out the back. This memory – and the time I was introduced to Vegemite – will stay with me forever.

'Many years had passed before I saw a small oil painting of a chook at an exhibition in Geelong in 1986. I thought, I'd like to paint chooks one day. I started exhibiting in 1986. Since then I'd probably have to say I've painted and drawn hundreds of them. More miniatures than large ones. They are in England, and all over Australia, including Tasmania.

'When I first started chooks were just the subject matter, then I decided to change direction and create characters out of them, almost caricatures of them. I try to tell a story with the chooks in the picture, and show how they relate to each other. I put words in their mouth; there's an interaction. I like being able to bring them to life. They have got character – so that's always in my mind.

'First, I drew them on paper, then in oils on canvas. My own chooks were my first subjects. I've now had chooks for thirty years. I currently have four brown chooks. I've no idea what breed they are, and I like all colours and breeds, particularly the black ones, as bright violets, turquoise and viridian shimmer in their plumage in the full sunlight. They supply the most incredibly yummy eggs and we never eat the chooks. They don't have names; they are just all my girls. They have names in my paintings and sculptures though – Henny, Gertie, Mopar, Cordelia, Juliet, Lavinia, Miranda, Bianca, Boyet and rooster Claudius to name just a few.

'People who know me say, "Kris, you've made them your own." I've given them a contemporary look, made them a bit quirkier. Their personalities are what I'm interested in. They're pretty cute. I love the way they scratch around then turn their heads to look at where they've just scratched. I feed them goodies – raisins or seeds. One chook jumped up onto the table next to me, up close and personal, it was a great opportunity to draw her feet. Now people give me photos of chooks, and I still take some photos as well. I like roosters but I don't like them around my girls. I like them to have peace.

'I'm grateful to the chook fanatics out there who've kept the whole process happening. It's given me the chance to bring something new to the table. We need the collectors out there; we do what meets the need to be creative. Without collectors we'd all end up with a heap of paintings lying around. So many people have said to me, "We love chooks." Two sisters at an exhibition, both old maids, were funny. One was saying how she loved chooks and the other said, "Well, I hate them, and I would never hang a chook painting on my wall. Our rooster always terrorised and chased me."'

At this point Kris's husband Doug walked into the kitchen. He was home from work for lunch. 'He's my right-hand man.' Naturally, I want to know Doug's thoughts on Kristina's chooks. It is soon obvious that he is her number one fan.

'She's pretty brilliant, actually. She'll put a piece of material aside, and I'll say, "What d'you want to keep that for?" Then she goes and creates something, so I tend to keep quiet now. Her art brings a lot of activity here – and excitement. I don't mind the chooks; they've been very good to us. I'm her fetch-and-carry man, especially the heavy stuff. I help move the works to and from exhibitions.'

Kristina is very effusive about her husband, too. She tells me later that they always have been close, and never more so than since he got over a prostate cancer operation.

Kristina relates how good Doug is technically. 'He built the first studio and fitted out the second one. I went to sculptural welding classes for three years to learn all sorts of processes in welding and metal cutting, trying to fine-tune my skills. One day Doug decided that we should fix a wheelbarrow, and I said, "I'm the welder in the family so I'll do the welding." Anyway, after I'd made a botch of it Doug took over and welded it perfectly, without any lessons. He's a natural at problem solving and anything technical.'

The Brownings have been married for thirty-six years. And art runs in the family. Daughter Sonia, thirty-two, is an artist in Perth, as is her man Glenn. Kristina and Doug's son, Nathan, thirty, and his wife Laura live in Sunbury. Nathan is on tree maintenance for the Hume Council and he has a passion for welding, too. Sonia, Glenn and Nathan all exhibited their work with Kristina at the Castlemaine State Festival. Nathan made brightly coloured welded metal bathing boxes and a wild west saloon; Sonia's works were acrylics on paper; while Glenn, a surrealist painter, created acrylics on large canvases, with both Sonia and Glenn exhibiting printmaking.

Doug continues his thoughts on Kris's place in the art world. 'It's been a pretty exciting career for Kris. She's run with it 100 per cent. She's always been talented, even as a kid at school. It's been a big part of my life too. I've supported her and try to help her as much as I can when I'm needed.'

Kristina cuts in, 'Except with the chainsaw. That went down like a lead balloon.'

'Oh that,' he says. Seems that when Kristina decided she

wanted to go into 3D art she thought carving with a chainsaw might be good, and sought Doug's help to learn how to use one, but Doug was having none of that. He thought she'd cut her leg off. Once this was off the agenda a new medium to express 3D art forms needed to be considered.

We continued to chat, but soon it was time for Doug to go back to work. He works in the engineering office at FlowServe (known for many years as Thompsons Foundry) in Castlemaine; and he's been there for forty-three years. So we shake hands and look forward to meeting up again. He seems like a nice, quiet and steady bloke.

I asked Kristina to tell me something about her family background. I was searching for a historic link with art, I suppose. 'Well, I was born to a German mum and a Polish dad; they met and lived in Lubeck, Germany after the war. They wanted to make a new start, so with little twelve-month-old Barbara in tow (and Mum pregnant with me) they sailed off to Australia and arrived here in 1950.

'As assisted passengers they were sent to Bonegilla Migrant Camp. But this had no facilities for pregnant women, and as Mum was soon to have me, they were sent to Rushworth Migrant Camp. It was awful, according to Mum: huts only had crudely made partition walls. Dad eventually put up blankets to make it warmer and more private. He was then sent to work at Cairn Curran reservoir to help build the dam. Eventually they moved into a miner's cottage in Campbells Creek. It was a very small cottage, and they had to share it with another family. We were there until I was five. Then we moved into a rented terrace building in Castlemaine. Dad converted the apartments and we ended up with three outside loos and it was so old it had a demolition order on it, but they got it for £1 a week, and we lived there until I was a teenager.

'I met Doug in 1967 when I was just seventeen. I was working for Sandhurst Dairies as a typist clerk – mainly counting milk bottles. I used to look out the window and see the garage across the road and thought how much fun it would be to work there. Luckily the woman who had that job fell pregnant, and due to health and safety rules you weren't allowed to do that job while pregnant so I got the job and worked as a typist clerk, but also as the driveway attendant, pulling petrol and selling batteries. I loved it, I just loved it. Doug and I were married in 1970. We rented a place from Thompsons, and later built a home at Campbells Creek.

'I gave up painting when the kids were young, and did some part-time jobs. I regret not carrying it on, but I gave it away until I could concentrate on it without interruption – it was difficult using oils with little kids around. Finally in 1983 I attended realist art classes in Bendigo, part time. By 1986 I started to exhibit my work. Mum and Dad gave me a box of Faber-Castell Polychromos pencils for my thirty-seventh birthday, so I did watercolour classes to learn their principles, which also apply to pencils as well.

'In 1992 I started teaching drawing skills to budding artists in the studio, and then in 1995 went on to study fine art at Ballarat University, gaining my Bachelor of Arts degree, majoring in drawing. It was a real commitment to travel over to Ballarat five days a week, but it was all worth it, and it was satisfying to graduate as a mature-age student in 1997.

'I had put my passion for coloured pencil work on the back burner at this time. I studied printmaking as an elective at university, which drove me to investigate it further. So printmaking became a real passion. I enjoyed working with copper, zinc and aluminium plates. As Doug wouldn't teach me how to use a chainsaw, and as I had enjoyed working with metal while printmaking, I decided I might enjoy welding. I started a course at Bendigo Regional Institute of Technology at the Castlemaine campus in 2001, and stayed there learning everything I could until I had completed all of the modules in the course and they kicked me out in 2004. It was a part-time course, but it taught me all I needed to know about welding. We even did a little blacksmithing in the course.

'By 2004 we had set everything up here at home. Doug built the first studio in 1992 for my drawing and teaching, and fitted out the second studio in 1997 for printmaking and framing, and then in 2003 I took over the patio for my welding. Now my work is dominated by those three areas. The coloured pencil chooks have definitely developed over the years and printmaking is still a very important part of my overall work, I have developed a series of works titled 'Japanese-inspired monotype printmaking', which is new, and that's what I go for – originality. My son had been fighting bushfires, and as I watched it on the news I was inspired to do a *Bushfire* series, and then went on to a *Summer* series when Mum died. The prints I now produce are a direct development of these series of events. And then, of course, my welding is a real passion; I love welding.'

Kristina is a permanent artist on exhibition at Wilson's Gallery at Robe, in South Australia. She also receives visitors into her studios in Campbells Creek, which adjoins Castlemaine and every two years she cleans out the studios and throws open the doors for a full-on exhibition as an umbrella event during the Castlemaine State Festival. Titles of some of the chook drawings for this year's exhibition include 'The Broody Bunch', 'Alter Ego' and 'Happy Homemakers'.

I love chooks as well, and was telling her about our two – Henrietta and Esmeralda. Sadly old Henrietta died two days ago, after spending nine years in our backyard. Esmeralda soldiers on.

It was time to leave the chook lady, but we shall meet again. Before I left I wanted her to tell me what it all meant to her. I could see a real professionalism in her attitude as well as real passion.

As for the chooks – 'I'm always looking at portraying and doing them differently. And for me they are an everlasting inspiration as a subject.' And her art – 'I feel blessed to be given a gift and doubly blessed to be given the opportunity to follow my dreams.'

Sparra from Yarra

RAY WEYGOOD

'THE TRANSPORT REGULATION BOARD WAS FULL OF POMS AND
IRISH INSPECTORS — NO AUSSIE WOULD BE SO TOUGH ON
HIS FELLOW MAN.'

There was probably no other business that Ray 'Sparra' Weygood was going to end up in other than transport. His grandfather was a truckie and his father was a truckie, and so Ray became a truckie, as did two of his own sons. His grandfather, Charles Richard Weygood, born at Harden, New South Wales, became a railway fettler, and later bought a truck and was contracted to help put a railway tunnel through at the New South Wales town of Bethungra. He started his business, C.R. Weygood, at Morundah in New South Wales in 1924.

His wife had died just six weeks after giving birth to son Cyril Richard in 1910. The young boy was placed in the hands of relatives and his father started a new life. Years later, when Cyril was just eighteen, he went into the trucking business, in opposition to his long-lost father. In 1924 they renewed their contact, and soon the two reunited as a family.

In 1932 young Cyril took over the family business. The work mainly involved road making. There is a photo of Cyril with a truckload of long wood poles he had cut himself. He had a contract to take the poles and install them as telephone lines out to a station, 11 miles from Morundah. He had to dig the 36-inch holes for each pole, drop the poles in and then install the wooden cross-arms to carry the line. He also installed the insulators and the wire. Inspectors were tough and took delight in filling in holes if they weren't deep enough and making you re-dig the hole.

Later on he operated the business as primarily livestock cartage. In 1958 Cyril moved from Morundah and by then was operating nineteen stock crates for livestock cartage. Cyril's son Ray, widely known as Sparra, has been a truckie for fifty-two years and I found him at his trucking depot in Yarrawonga. 'My dad was called "Sparrow" (Sparra), and I've been called it since I was about four. I guess because I was small in height like my dad. My sons are "little sparras" and my grandkids are "baby sparrows".'

Sparra has finally retired and sold off the trucks, and his huge shed is now filled with large containers of olives in water – it's now a space rented out to another company. The trucks are all gone except one. Sparra retired in May 2006, and is just finalising all his life's work.

'I bought my first truck in 1954, a AS160 International I called "Miss Delma". In those days we carried fodder to outstations and brought back wool to the railway stations. We weren't allowed to compete with the railways so we couldn't cart direct to Melbourne or anywhere else the railways were headed. In

1955 I had a 28-foot long stock crate which was equivalent to one and a half railway trucks. I could carry 160 sheep in it, but we were only allowed to carry them to local markets, and only to Newmarket in Melbourne if there weren't any railway trucks available. By 1960 they allowed some road carrying, but we were never allowed to carry on Sundays. Usually it was okay to carry stock from farms to the sale yards. The government had formed the Transport Regulation Board (TRB) to regulate all transport movements. The TRB was full of Poms and Irish inspectors – no Aussie would be so tough on his fellow man – but they didn't care and they were bloody tough on truckies. No wonder most of the unions are now full of the Poms and the Irish. They made it very hard to operate. We also carried a lot of bulk wheat and baled hay off the farm paddocks to the sheds, and wool to the railways and then to Melbourne.

'By 1960 we had nineteen trucks towing 38-foot long stock crates. Sixteen were triple-deckers and three were double-deckers. Dad would buy four trucks at a time. By the 1970s we had moved into Atkinson and Ford trucks. We always built our own stock crates. By the 1970s it was okay for border towns like us to operate interstate and transport over the border, so we started doing a lot of interstate work. In 1975 and '76 stock jobs deteriorated so we diversified into general carrying interstate and joined up with Border Express, who at that time only had twelve trucks. Now they have probably 300 trucks on the road. We had been in operations with Border Express from 1974 right through until I ceased operations in May 2006.

'When we went into interstate operations we did a lot of carrying of Tubemakers' pipes from Sydney, and carted with six LTL Ford trucks, taking pipes to Perth, Mt Tom Price, Port Hedland, Meekatharra, Roxby Downs – all for work that was happening when mining was developing and expanding. We were carrying pipes between 1980 and 1992.

'The first time we crossed the Nullabor was in 1956 when we took the first merino breeding ewes from Tubbo Station to Esperance. We took a thousand head over in five trucks. The Nullabor in those days was very different – the bit of bitumen we saw was in the towns, the rest of it was dirt – probably 90 per cent of the trip was on rough gravel and sand. The sheep were quarantined at Port Augusta for a couple of days before we were allowed to enter Western Australia. The sheep had to be shorn six weeks earlier and carry no burrs. We mainly drove at night as the dust was so heavy during the heat of the day and it hung in the sky. At night the Nullabor got so cold but the dew on the ground kept the dust down. We only lost ten sheep over the whole trip. We had two drivers in each truck and kept going as much as possible, depending on the heat of the day.

'The Nullabor then was more interesting than now. We had fuel in 44-gallon drums; there were no service stations like now. The Caltex Nundaroo depot run by George Chick had fuel in 44-gallon drums that had to be hand-pumped into the trucks. He also had a roadside dump 200 miles further on down the track at the rabbit-proof fence between Nundaroo and the border. Another spot – Ivy Tank – is bypassed now on the new road. Reg Gurney operated another stop at the Golden Fleece depot at Eucla. It would usually take five days to travel across from Port Augusta. We only travelled up to Darwin once and that was for a one-off load of pipes, and we brought a load of watermelons back from Kununurra. The last time I drove across the Nullabor was four years ago – all those flash roadhouses and wide bitumen roads – very different to the old days.

'I'd hate to say how many sheep we moved over the years – millions, I suppose. One triple-decker stock-truck could carry 420 lambs, multiply that by many, many trucks over fifty-odd years and you get an idea.

'Much of our sheep work was to and from salesyards at Jerilderie, Lockhart, Wee Waa, Narromine, Trangie, Coolamon, Naracoorte, Bairnsdale and many other places. Yarrawonga became a big centre. At our peak in the 1960s we had twenty-five employees – they earned £20 a week plus tucker. In 1960 you could buy a Comer truck for £2800 and petrol was one-and-sixpence a gallon. Today the latest Stirling truck costs $220 000 and diesel fuel is the equivalent of $6 a gallon. Truckies earn about $1200 gross a week.

'In March 1993 we started carting other sorts of stock. We carried twenty-four adult emus from Western Australia to Wilby. In 1998 we carted the first load of emus and ostriches from Western Australia across the Nullabor. Between 1999 and 2003 we moved 30 000. They were in open semitrailers with a tarp over the top. We later carried ten camels from Port Augusta to Beechworth. In 2000 it was fifteen loads of emus to Tasmania, we've also taken loads of buffalo and fallow deer.

'I guess the best truck I had over the years was a 1960s L190 International. The worst was probably the latest Stirling truck; we had three blow up in 2004. In the old days you'd have a truck do a million miles and there'd be no problems. Mind you, the old trucks had none of the latest luxuries like power steering or air conditioning. They also had very dim headlights. Trips in the old days were very different, too. It took seven hours to drive from Yarrawonga to Melbourne. We did a lot of miles in later years carrying stock to Newmarket salesyards in Melbourne, and to meat processors like Borthwicks, Angliss, Wagstaff and

Gilbertsons. The Newmarket salesyards were a tremendous institution, now they are all gone and housing estates cover them.

'The good years are long gone. It has been a hard life and it's getting tougher to operate independently. Nowadays most freight to Western Australia is carried in large containers on long trains; the trains are now huge business and are run by huge companies. The transport industry has been going downhill for many years.'

So after fifty-four years as a truckie and family business operator, Sparra has other interests to fill up his day. In 1978 he bought the local milk lorry and horse and drove it around town for a laugh. He gave kids rides whenever they wanted, taking them to school and such, and the interest grew. He bought the kids their own horses, and finally he and wife Delma created Bindi Hill on 10 acres at Mulwala, a place where troubled kids could take time out, ride horses, go camping and enjoy the bush life.

Since then, kids from Yarrawonga, Beechworth, Rutherglen and even Melbourne over the years have enjoyed time at Bindi Hill. 'Some of the kids had tough home lives and so we gave them and their parents a break.' The success of the enterprise has been very evident, especially when the children decided to give Sparra and Delma a reunion. Two-hundred and fifty kids, now adults in their forties with their own kids, turned up in May 2003. Bindi Hill still operates, bringing a great deal of joy after all these years. Five children from one family, daughters of one of the original kids, still attend. Bindi Hill is a special place for the many people with fond memories of the kindness and efforts of the Weygood family.

'All we could give them was love and affection and horses and somewhere for the kids to get away from it all for a while and have fun.'

Sparra is also a member of the 'Whereabouts' group – ex-members of the Draught Horse Association, made up of people who have a love of the grand old draught horse. They also love their gypsy wagons; Ray had a beautiful wagon built to his own design. The group meet once a month, and every September for three weeks each year travel and camp in various parts of the country. This year Sparra travelled over 600 kilometres with his wagon towed by his clydesdales Mac and Lager, and was accompanied by his little Jack Russell terrier Clancy. His route was from Yarrawonga to Kybram, Mitiamo, Pyramid Hill, Cohuna, Deniliquin, Mathoura, Barmah, Wakool and back home.

'My wife loathes horses and won't have a bar of it all, but Clancy absolutely loves to travel with me. I don't do it tough – the wagon, whilst looking like a real old-time gypsy wagon, is decked out with the latest gear: a microwave, solar panels, refrigerator, colour TV, CD/DVD player, twin-system air conditioning, George Foreman grill, electric jug and toaster, and, of course, a double bed. It costs me 50 cents a kilometre: $60 a week in horse chaff. A set of horse shoes last 300 kilometres and costs $200 to replace. Not only do the horses tow the gypsy wagon, but a small matching trailer, too, as well as a small lorry to give kids a ride on.'

Now that he has more time Sparra intends to be away two out of every four weeks. His next major trip is to follow the folk festivals – Wangaratta Blues, Harrietville Bluegrass, Barmah Country, and El Dorado. He will be away for a month over November/December, enjoying the music and his horses. Usually six wagons travel with him, and they do about 30 kilometres a day. They carry their own water and food for the horses. He stops every two hours to give the horses a drink: they get through 40 litres a day. Next year Sparra has a trip planned to go to Deniliquin, Conargo and up to Hay and beyond.

All this is pretty amazing for a man who has lost most of his sight. 'Dad started to lose his sight when he was in his fifties, and I've been the same. I could probably get something done about my eyes, but I've never been to a doctor in my life – they terrify me – so I just continue on and make the best of it.' Sparra believes his and his father's eyesight failing may be as a result of years of dust and chemicals. 'We dealt with them so much on a daily basis – with foot-rot baths for sheep at yards, and field bins were always cleaned out with chemicals, toxins to kill weevils and such. Dad died in 1991 aged eighty-four. He had bad vision for many years. Mine has been deteriorating for twenty years.'

Sparra can still make out outlines of people, and read large print up close, but he says he listens for noises before he crosses the road. He says there's no worry about driving the horses; they are very smart and know what they are doing. His granddaughter has helped as she does a lot of travelling, too. Sparra likes to be behind the reins and still feels very confident at what he does. He and his wife Delma have been married for forty-seven years, and they have four children and eight grandchildren to keep them busy.

'You just learn to live with it and get on with life,' he says matter-of-factly.

He says the horses and travelling is a great way to spend the rest of his days.

Grey Power

LAURIE & BEV WOLTERS
'THERE IS NO FREEDOM LIKE THE OPEN ROAD.'

I saw them coming in the distance, and I knew by the look of their set-up that they were serious about travel. Queenslanders heading north, home for Christmas after eight months on the road, and me heading south. They are just two of many Australians who see the open road as a way of life. They might not live permanently in the bush, but these two active people in their seventies have boiled the billy in more bush places and travelled more miles than many. They have a deep appreciation for their country.

'We often get lost,' laughs Bev.

'Not lost – just confused,' says Laurie, 'and we get to change our neighbours whenever we want to.'

We sat under a gum tree in their motor-home, having a yarn and a cuppa. Bev continued to crochet one of her beautiful

253

rugs. It helps to pass the miles away. We met again a further hundred miles up the road the next day to continue our yarn as we each had more time.

Laurie Wolters is a retired Australian Army Major. Originally he was a tracer for Melbourne Metropolitan Board of Works, and later worked as a draftsman, before joining the army. He and his wife Bev lived in Victoria, but Queensland has been home for many years. Over the twenty years Laurie was in the army, they lived at Balcombe on Victoria's Mornington Peninsula; in Ingleburn, New South Wales; and in Canungra and Brisbane, Queensland. Laurie also spent 1966–67 in Vietnam with RAME 101 Field Workshop. In later years they spent some time in Singapore. After he retired from the army in 1979, Laurie worked as a secretary of a golf club, for McWilliams Wines, as a real estate agent, and a rice tester.

Whenever they leave their Queensland home for one of their many long trips away, the space underneath the seats of their home on wheels is jammed full with home-made wooden toys that Laurie and Bev Wolters sell all over Australia.

'It helps to defray the costs of travel,' says Laurie. I can tell they really only go home to water the garden, make a load of toys, and then head off again.

'I'd rather make toys than do housework,' says Bev. 'When we get home we clean up the yard, do what we have to. I hate unpacking the motor-home and washing. I love the garden – and bingo two nights a week.'

It's a team effort, this making toys. Whilst Bev will get in and help cut things out on the band saw, her main job is varnishing and painting. 'I don't do sanding,' she says. They make the toys in the workshop underneath their house, and they include a range of trucks, racing cars, Mini Minors, sedans, school buses, road trains and other pieces. 'We sell them to kindergartens, child-care centres, preschools and anyone who wants them,' says Laurie. 'Often we'll then get grandmothers ringing us and saying they saw the toys at a school and asking us to send this and that, and we do – all over Australia. We've been doing it for ten years or more. It's good to see the smiles on the kids' faces.'

'Laurie is the salesman, and I'm the packhorse that helps carry them into the schools,' laughs Bev.

I asked about some of the places they'd sold their items to and immediately you know this couple have travelled some miles. 'Dirranbandi, Charleville, St George, Roma, Winton, Cootamundra, Parkes, Cowra, Hay, Culcairn, Wellington, Alice Springs, Mt Gambier, Perth – often we run out of stuff. We even give some schools time to pay – you can trust the Australian outback,' says Laurie.

On their way home, the toys underneath the seats and in the cupboards are replaced with another collection: wine. 'At home we drink chateau cardboard, but on the road we try all sorts of wineries and enjoy a red at night with our meal,' says Laurie, and on this trip they are taking quite a few bottles home with them from various wineries all over Australia. It seems like a pretty good lifestyle.

It all started years ago when they bought a caravan so they would have something to travel in when they went to Victoria from Queensland to see relatives and friends. 'We had the caravan behind a Nissan four-wheel drive from 1982–84 and did some 25 000 kilometres. Then from 1984 to 1996 we had a HJ75 Toyota Landcruiser and caravan, and also did some tenting for a while and covered 248 000 kilometres.'

I ask how the motor-home got the name 'Our Pipe Dream', which is written in big letters across the top on front of the van. Bev replied, 'We were in a motel in Longreach, we had a four-wheel drive at the time, and here was Laurie drooling over a big motor-home parked on the street. I said, "If you ever get one of those it will be one of your pipe dreams."'

The 1985 Toyota Dyna is fitted with a Sunchaser body. It does 5 kilometres a litre travelling at their usual 85 kilometres an hour. They got it in 1996 and it now has 185 000 kilometres on it. They have done over 17 000 kilometres on this eight-month trip. I told them I'd not long returned from doing 14 374 kilometres in just twenty days, crossing Australia twice with a mate! But we weren't just cruising on holidays, we were testing a ute just for an excuse to go bush!

On a trailer behind the motor-home is Bev and Laurie's little 1994 Suzuki panel van. They use it as a day vehicle to go exploring away from the motor-home, in places up to 100 kilometres away. 'It's been very convenient, allowed us to do more,' says Laurie, as he sips his tea.

'We have a UHF/CB which we use all the time, talk a lot to the truckies. If I see one coming up behind me I usually give them right of way to pass me and say "When you're ready, big wheels – it's your job, my pleasure."'

'Sometimes we have "freebies", where we just camp beside the road. We are members of the Campervan and Motorhome Club Australia and we meet up with a lot of other motor-home owners at rallies twice a year. We just had one at Barcaldine, where there were approximately 1000 motor-homes. The rallies are great; they have entertainment, workshops on things like first aid, cooking, and other technical seminars. And of course we sit around drinking and telling lies,' says Laurie. 'We've been to rallies in Townsville, Forbes, Warragul, Alice Springs, Latrobe, Northam – all over Australia.

'Bev gets fearful whenever I bring the road maps out,' he says with a laugh. 'She knows I'm planning around the motor-home rallies and looking for places we've not seen before or areas people have told us about, or where we want to see again.' 'I don't drive at all,' says Bev. 'I don't have a licence; I did years ago. I don't like the city traffic.'

'But she's my co-pilot,' says Laurie. 'My co-pilot looks after me; there's nothing I want for.'

Luckily, nothing bad has ever happened on their trips. 'Some mechanical defects, but that's part of it all,' says Laurie. 'I enjoy the road, seeing new territory, the vegetation, the sunsets, particularly, and sitting around talking to people. I can see the beauty in red dirt. I just enjoy the road and other road users.'

For Bev, too, the appeal is 'meeting lots of new people, seeing new places. We've got acquaintances all over Australia and it's lovely to meet up at rallies. I like to photograph all the flowers. The wildflowers of Western Australia, particularly, the wreath flowers at Mullewa are something special. I loved Kalbarri in Western Australia, the Bungle Bungles, Lake Argyle, and the beaches. Absolutely fascinating. I'm a beachcomber; I love just walking the beaches collecting shells, watching dolphins play in the water.'

Laurie cuts in. 'There are better places than Monkey Mia to see dolphins though, which we thought was a rip-off, and we'd never go back there again. Too commercial.'

Bev continues, 'The Bungle Bungles are so completely different. We went in a chopper flight over it first, then went in by four-wheel drive – well worth the effort.'

'It makes you proud to be an Australian. No other places in the world have got what we have,' Laurie adds.

Other memories come back to Bev – 'The Pinnacles in Western Australia are incredibly beautiful and different.' And they both agree that the HMAS *Sydney* Memorial at Geraldton was special. 'It really got to us. Very, very moving – nothing else quite like it.' Other places that have really impressed include the township of Burra in South Australia, Gulgong in New South Wales and Western Australia's Lake Argyle. And the Wolters thought the Kimberley was breathtaking, with its 'ever-changing colours'.

But Western Australia and the Northern Territory also have other memories for Bev, they can be difficult places: 'Lots and lots of miles between places, and some places, like Arnhem Land, can be rough in bits.' Laurie likes the bush, though. But for the Wolters some places have 'lost their magic', as Laurie puts it. Port Douglas, for instance, was 'just a little village, but development has spoilt it and now it's over-commercialised.'

Laurie likes to describe Australia this way – 'There's a geographical feature called the Great Dividing Range which goes from the tip of Queensland to Victoria. On the east side of this range is some land and on the west side is the real Australia. Out west the people are magic.'

They have been on so many trips to so many parts of Australia it is impossible to list all of them, but some of their best memories include a four-wheel drive trip, organised by the Queensland Geographical Society, with about seventeen other vehicles called 'In the steps of Leichhardt the explorer' – through Queensland, Northern Territory and Western Australia.

Another was 'From Brisbane to the Tip' – up to Cape York Peninsula then home.

'We have camped in many nice places by the sea such as Cosy Corner Tasmania, Coronation Beach and Kalbarri, Western Australia,' says Laurie, 'also Wonga Beach, Queensland and Bawley Point, New South Wales. Inland areas which come to mind are the Granites (north of Mount Magnet), Lake Argyle, Dryandra Woodlands – all in Western Australia. Haslem, Wilpena Pound, Wannon Falls all in South Australia.'

For a long time the Wolters also enjoyed gem fossicking for stones like opals, topaz and sapphires at places like White Cliffs, Duck Creek, Lightning Ridge, O'Brien's Creek, Torrington, Rubyvale, Tomahawk Creek, Eromanga and Nullamanna.

They can't understand why people travel overseas before seeing Australia. They describe themselves as 'Australians through and through'.

And so I left them to travel on, knowing the grass won't grow under their feet too long before they'll be moving on yet again. We'll probably meet on the road 'out there' again one day. I couldn't agree more when Laurie says that seeing Australia is 'something you must do if you can'.

Birdman of the Bush

BRUCE STEPHENS

'BY BREEDING BIRDS IN CAPTIVITY, HOPEFULLY WE'LL LEAVE OUR
KIDS WITH SOME SPECIES THAT WOULD OTHERWISE DISAPPEAR.'

Growing up in the bush years ago was tough. Bruce Stephens'
father, who was brought up on a farm at Mittyack in north-
west Victoria, used to say how he didn't wear shoes until
he was twelve years old. He died a couple of years ago aged
eighty-seven, so a tough outdoor life didn't hurt him. Receipts
kept by his son Bruce show that his father earnt over £20 for
one month – June 1936 – a lot of money in those days, for selling rabbits and foxes to a local dealer. It was at the end of the
Depression and people in the bush were resourceful, surviving
the best way they could. Obviously, Bruce's father knew what
hard yakka was.

Bruce Stephens was always surrounded by animals, particularly birds. His parents, Jean and Jack, owned a chook farm and
had many sheds on the property. With one brother and two

sisters in the family, it was Bruce who took his interest in birds to a serious level. By the time he was in his late teens he was known as 'bird boy', and was the feature of a two-page colour story in his local paper.

Bruce started to collect birds when he was just ten years old; he always brought home the sick or injured magpies he'd find on the side of the road. Between the ages of ten and eighteen he owned budgies, finches, parrots and rosellas, regent parrots and pheasants. Pheasants! At one stage he had 200 pheasants of all varieties, including many for sale as pets and some for eating. Hawks and eagles were also two of his favourite birds. 'When the chooks were cut back by my parents at one stage there were plenty of places for me to keep birds – in the many chook sheds on the property. I also got to use some of the chook food to feed them, so I guess my Dad sponsored me – well, he paid for some of the food, anyway. In those days if you could keep pheasants alive you were doing well. I used to advertise in the *Weekly Times* and sell them. I'd get the equivalent of $5 a pair for pheasants; the same birds now fetch $100. I was always interested in them.'

From the age of eighteen Bruce had a spell away from buying and breeding birds. Work kept him busy, and at the time it was certainly not fashionable for your mates to know you had them. He also became interested in the other type of bird – the female variety without feathers.

A few months ago the family home and land were sold, and a new church and school will be built on the site, so the chook sheds are no longer. The surrounding land is no longer paddocks but a thriving housing estate. Bruce has moved on and now lives on his own 40 acres, where he is very much surrounded by animals – not just birds, but deer and goats, too.

The drought has hit hard like everywhere, so instead of the 200 deer he once owned, Bruce is down to twenty.

When he left school in 1968 Bruce drove a water truck for an excavation contractor, who was building a large reservoir at Mt Korong to stop erosion. Later he worked for a bookshop as a storeman driver. Then he had a year as a storeman in an egg producers' co-op, followed by a stint on a dairy farm, which he found was practically slave labour. Back to life as a storeman, he worked for an electronics place for two years and then joined the SEC (State Electricity Commission). There he worked as a storeman for five years, and then as a meter reader for the next twenty years, a job which kept him outdoors but also on the road travelling all over Victoria.

His job took him to towns ranging from Charlton, Inglewood, Bridgewater, Tarnagulla, Newbridge, St Arnaud and Marnoo, back towards Maryborough, Castlemaine, Macedon, Woodend, Gisborne, Trentham and Daylesford and across to Riddell's Creek, Romsey, Lancefield, Hesket, Hanging Rock and Heathcote. In other words, Bruce has seen a lot of country Victoria.

Many of the jobs were day trips, others were overnight trips. Bruce would often have one day in each town and so trips away could last up to ten days. The job not only meant reading meters in country towns but also on farms, where water pumps could be anywhere. Often it was a case of following mud maps to locate them, especially if property owners were unavailable.

In 1999 Bruce took a package from SEC, as it had become Powercor and many of the jobs were made redundant or were being contracted out. As he had land with a lot of dry timber on it, Bruce spent six months cutting wood and selling firewood to people in the district. It was a welcome break being home and being able to finish off renovating his farm house.

In 2000 he separated from his wife and began a new life. Birds were well and truly back on the scene, and Bruce's many sheds for them kept him busy breeding. He also began a new job as a sub-contractor, erecting sheds of all sorts for Ranbuild, and coincidentally that job has now taken Bruce on the road back to many of those towns he serviced as an SEC meter reader. 'The boss doesn't have to give me too many directions; I usually know exactly where to go as I've been to most of the areas many times before. It's good; I am pretty well my own boss and a mate works with me, so I work my own hours. I enjoy the outdoor life, except for the extremes of the weather sometimes. Roofing iron when it's too cold or too hot to pick up sometimes is a pain. I've been doing it for seven years now.

'My daughter Shioban is back in Bendigo now after finishing university in Melbourne. She works at the uni as a student information officer. She is twenty-six now, and engaged to be married this year. She is great. She did a sports science degree and then taught at uni in Melbourne. She later worked with the Victorian Sports Institute and also the Victory soccer team. She has run programs in sports science for elite athletes. Actually, she is an elite athlete herself and has represented Australia in three sports – gymnastics, tumbling and diving. Unfortunately the week they chose athletes for the Melbourne Commonwealth Games she broke a toe and missed out, which was a pity. She is pretty switched on and has turned out pretty well – she's a good kid.' I detected that Bruce was actually pretty damned proud of his daughter and they sounded close.

I first met the birdman of the bush a few years ago and knew then that I'd be back to interview him. I had come to see Bruce

at his pretty farm, and to see and hear more of his birds. Bruce and I discussed the hobby of keeping and breeding Australian native birds. While it's a hobby that can be done on the cheap, it can also get quite expensive; either way it is enjoyable. When you have a Category 3 Private Advanced Licence like Bruce has the main cost is buying the birds themselves. For instance, a pair of red-rumped parrots (commonly called grassies) costs only between $10 and $30, depending on the colour mutations; whereas red-tailed black cockatoos cost $3500 a pair. Keeping birds is like growing roses – the rarer the colour and quality the more you'll pay.

Bruce has a wide range of birds and an even wider range in colour mutations. He is a dedicated breeder. At the time I visited him it was a hot 30 degree day, with the whole district covered in smoke from the north-eastern Victorian fires. As a man on the land, Bruce keeps an eye on smoke and is wary on days like this. Bruce's collection of birds at the moment consists of four red-tailed black cockatoos; six major mitchell cockatoos, two sulphur-crested cockatoos, five galahs, twenty Indian red-necked parrots, two eclectus (found only in a tiny part of far northern Australia and in New Guinea), two mallee ring-necked parrots, two eastern rosellas, and thirty red-rumped parrots, ranging from bright yellow with a blood red-spotted back to just about every colour of the rainbow.

'The red-tailed black cockatoos are my favourites – they are a spectacular bird and the hardest of all to breed in captivity. I have two pairs for breeding, but they haven't produced young in four years; we are continually hoping to see them become parents. They aren't birds who'll rear their own easily. I have raised some here previously that were here on agistment. Getting adults birds that are compatible is the biggest issue, more so than with any other bird. While there aren't a lot in the wild, they are still out there and hopefully they'll grow in numbers again. They are expensive, and you can't buy them easily. It's hard to buy a hen – and not everyone can afford $3500 for a pair. For me, they are the ultimate Australian bird. I would love a pair of South American macaws. Would you believe 30 000 macaws were exported to the United States in one year?

'The colour and scarcity adds to the cost: the rarer the bird, the dearer the licence. The princess parrot is virtually extinct in the wild, and in captivity they breed freely and do not require a licence to keep – they are that common. Other birds that are numerous and breed easily you don't have to pay as much for. The licence I have covers just about every Australian bird. It costs you $129 each year and you're supplied with a detailed record book. You are required to submit details annually and can be inspected on site by the Department of Sustainability and Environment anytime they want. If you keep good records and do what's required, you shouldn't be worried about that, though. In the record book you have to note every bird you own, who it was bought from and their licence details, and also any births or deaths of birds and all sales and purchases as well. You cannot take birds from the wild, or buy or sell eggs. Some people have licences to supply sulphur-crested cockatoos and galahs for the pet trade.

'At the moment the hobby is a bit more expensive because of the drought. The seed is about five times dearer than it normally is. I also collect green feed and such for them. I found out that they absolutely love celery. They love wild milk thistles and some grasses, too, but of course they always have bought seed and water at their disposal for when they feel like it. They have nesting logs and log perches and cages big enough for them to fly up and down a fair way. The bigger the bird, the bigger the cage and shed. No small cages, so they're not forced to perch all day. The sheds that the cages are kept in are always locked to protect the birds. The main shed is fully insulated to reduce the influence of the weather. The birds can fly out of the heat or cold or go outside and perch in the sun. All my birds are well provided for. You learn about this game by reading. I have spent over thirty years collecting all sorts of reading material, and I still subscribe to a specialist magazine so I can learn more. Also, you learn by listening to other people who are doing the same hobby as yourself.

'By breeding birds in captivity, hopefully we'll leave our kids with some species that would otherwise disappear. Many of the hollow logs are disappearing in the wild and they're so important for them to breed in, as more and more housing estates creep into the bush and wipe out their territories, trees and such. Even old farm fences that have old hollows in them, mainly the strainer posts, are now being replaced by steel posts.'

As Bruce and I wandered from shed to shed, from cage to cage, looking at and discussing his birds I was amazed at the colour variations, and we discussed all sorts of things related to birds as I photographed. He also showed me his collection of Boer goats and deer in two paddocks. This is a man who really loves his animals. I was disappointed to find no dog, though. Without a doubt, for me the most spectacular of the birds were the red-tailed black cockatoos and the major mitchell cockatoos. I have the yellow-tailed black cockies near home, but to see these birds up close is truly a great experience. One major mitchell squawked at me endlessly. 'You'd like to bite me, wouldn't you?' I said as I photographed her. 'She sure would,' said Bruce. 'She's a bit temperamental that one.'

I wanted to know what it was that Bruce got from his hobby, and what information he wants to pass on to the next generation.

'Relaxation is what I get. I can walk out there to my birds and check on them and it takes your mind off everything else in your life. To the next generation of young breeders, I'd say first, do your homework. By all means buy birds, but research and know that the birds you buy will have the best opportunity to survive and breed. Know that the hobby is frowned upon by some people who think of it as like keeping the birds in gaol – I don't believe that birds are that intelligent. Be prepared to look after your birds; you need to spend time every day with them – at least a minimum of one hour a day, and more in the breeding season each Spring when you'll need to be chasing seed, grass, thistles and be soaking seed for them and looking at any signs of special requirements for the young and such.

'Everyone who has got into bird breeding says it gets in your blood like a disease. But be prepared for the wife to try and put the brakes on the spending money a bit. My lovely new wife Gael is a nurse – a midwife in fact. I met her at the blood bank one day. We were married in 2006. She likes the birds, and with her being a midwife there's that potential asset with being able to hand-raise baby birds – that instinct of caring comes with a being a nurse.'

Bruce just laughed when I asked if Gael knew that she was going to be a bird midwife.

Somehow, I think next Spring she'll be in for a surprise.

Top Tip Treasures

RAY PEARCE & DEIRDRE OUTHRED

'NO BANK WOULD LEND ME ANYTHING; RECYCLING IS WHAT I'VE
ALWAYS DONE TO LIVE. EVERY NAIL HAS TO BE STRAIGHTENED.'

I saw a story in the *Weekly Times* that there was going to be
an exhibition by artists who only used materials they'd found
at the local tip. The photograph of Ray Pearce made up my
mind that it was worth going along to, so a few days later I was
among the small crowd looking at the exhibition of weird and
wonderful articles, ranging from an elephant float, to bathing
boxes, slot machines, a stretcher with a skeleton painted on it,
boats and a fantastically odd lighthouse. I made arrangements
to visit Ray at the mud-brick home he built in the bush and
shared with another professional artist, Deirdre.

Ray was born on Christmas Day, 1949 in Bendigo. His father
sold shoes at Crawford's Shoe Shop. Ray failed his art ceramics
course at the Bendigo Institute of Technology because it happened when he was called up to do national service – not part

of his plan at all. He was a conscientious objector. 'I didn't want to kill or be killed or fall into the process at all, so I registered as a conscientious objector. I sent $100 to the Save our Sons movement and they advised that I needed a letter from a minister to say I was pacifist and that I should make a mess of the medical. They also said that I should make sure my objection included details like that I smoked marijuana, my brother was an epileptic, I was deaf in one ear and that my trigger finger was three times its normal size.

'Because of all the uncertainty and stress, I neglected my studies. People thought I was a coward. It wasn't done out of any heroism. It was done out of truth and beauty. I didn't like authority after my tech school experience of being failed. Teachers did not have a lot of sympathy. So I left and took up pottery – Blind Cow Pottery – we had an old rented place for $5 a week in Flora Hill. It had no doors or windows and a cow lived in it. We installed a kerosene kiln, which was pretty dangerous. A mate Dave Edwards and I had a business as such and we did pretty well. They were good times and we sold mainly to Melbourne, then all over Australia. Things like casserole dishes, mugs, jewellery. Deirdre was wearing some beads that I'd made when I first met her. I also made dinnerware and garden sculptures. We made for places in Melbourne like the Craft Centre in Toorak Road, Gargoyles in Prahran, Ishka and Distlefink.

'Then I went back to do my course again and did the final year, which I passed easily. And I have made a living out of it for the last thirty years and never wanted to work for anyone. I love the firing – it's like Christmas when you fire a load of pottery. It's not a very good lifestyle dollar-wise but it's okay – I make about $16000 a year, but I just love the

excitement of creating. I've made my own kilns and learnt all sorts of things – the losses and the gems led me on to the next excitement. You get the post-kiln blues and you have to prepare beforehand for the losses – money was only for paying the bills. I did it all up until about five years ago. Most people would buy a whole load and pay cash on delivery. Now times have changed and they want it on consignment and you have to hassle them to get your money.

'Nowadays painting and drawing are my main loves and I never compromise for the dollars. I sell at my price. I eventually decided to go my own way. I'd been doing pottery for a living, but over the last five years I have devoted myself to a new start. Now I do exhibitions rather than sell to shops. It's made for emotions rather than stock just to make some money. I don't do any domestic wares at all. In between I do some work in vineyards. During the mid-1980s Deirdre and I both ended up in the old Abbotts Supply Co. building and rented it as a gallery for an artists' co-op. That's how we met.'

It was time for Deirdre to tell more of her early life over a cuppa. The day was warm and sun streamed through the window of their kitchen/dining room, and after some friendly greetings and pats, the two dogs were now sleeping at our feet.

'I come from Blackburn in Melbourne. The Depression affected my parents. My grandparents farmed at Rushworth and later had a poultry farm in Blackburn. My parents were pianists and singers, operatic and trained in the arts. Dad was an engineer for gas and fuel companies and designed kilns. I was the youngest of four children. Mum volunteered at Kew Cottages all her life. I won art prizes at school, and so was always interested.

'I went to work in a wool testing laboratory for Italian wool buyers, and later spent a year as a kindergarten assistant. Then back to the lab, this time a soil testing lab for a few years. My marriage broke down; we had four kids but lost one in infancy. She taught me strengths.

'I then moved to Bendigo in the early 1980s. I had children in school and I went to the Bendigo College of Advanced Education (BCAE) and did a three year full-time degree in Fine Arts. Ray and his artist cronies set up the gallery to independently produce shows and get rewards from the co-op. I heard of it while I was at BCAE and so I approached them. We all ended up renting the studio space, and outside college time we devoted ourselves to artwork. I was interested in exhibitions and needed to develop a body of work. I finally finished my art degree in 1987. I was then full time at Art Space. He was then doing about six to eight exhibitions a year and I bought this 16-acre bush block. It had a tin shed and a good dam. I was getting sick of Art Space; too many of the artists there relied on Ray and I to run it to make sure it paid the rent. We had a monthly lease. Ray and I even ended up living there on site. It was tenuous living and we could have been removed any time, and then a new brood took over and we camped out here and have been here ever since.'

Ray adds, 'We spent seven years living in the shed, and then in the early 1990s we built another shed by rummaging through skips at the rear of the Capitol Theatre they were renovating.'

By 1994 it was time for Ray and Deirdre to start building their own home – a two-storey mud-brick place. They made all the mud bricks themselves and spent two years getting all the materials they required.

'We just added to it as we had the cash,' says Deirdre. 'Ray had some savings; he'd lived in cheap hovels and saved money.'

I wanted to know more of Deirdre's art work. 'I'm at the start of my career now, I believe. The current "Tip of the Iceberg" exhibition is a great help; it's opened up new visions for the future for exhibitions and group shows. We've done all the work ourselves on limited funds.'

Ray explained more of how the rubbish tip exhibition came about. 'No bank would lend me anything; recycling is what I've always done to live. Every nail has to be straightened. We are very poor by normal standards but we've figured out how to get what we want. We are quite reconciled to it. If you're in great debt, you lose your life. We learnt of the life we wanted.' Deirdre adds, 'We are building a renovator's delight. We are at the point of consolidating, and it feels good. We are always adapting.'

'You've just got to give it a go, don't do what everyone sees as the "right thing",' says Deirdre.

Ray and Deirdre have that give-it-a-go attitude to their art. In 2000 they were asked to help a local company that makes floats for the famous annual Bendigo Easter Fair parade – the oldest continuously run procession in Australia.

Thousands travel to see the festivities every year, particularly to see the Chinese dragon, which is one of the longest and oldest in the world, and is normally housed at the marvellous Chinese Museum. At one meeting to revamp and add new colour to the procession, someone said, 'If only we could afford to have live elephants in the parade,' but at $5000 each, the cost was too much. Ray and Deirdre helped make a series of floats with any spare glue, wire and bits of cloth they had, and with the left over material they decided to secretly build an elephant for the committee to add to the parade. It was a difficult job, but it proved to be very popular.

'It was our first theatrical experience and people laughed at it all the way as we passed through the street,' said Deirdre. 'It is an eight-legged elephant called Linda, with people underneath it to hold her up and make her walk. People absolutely loved her; she had no message, she is just a whimsical creation – she even wears ugg boots! It takes an hour to assemble and dress her. We've had drunk people think she is real.

'Linda has an articulated trunk; her ears move, her tail wags and she even pisses. She can stand on one leg and talk to people in the crowd. It's all part of the floorshow.'

Now Linda's fame has spread, what started out as a bit of a secret joke has led Ray, Deirdre and Linda the elephant made of recycled bits and pieces to places they could not have imagined. Ray and Deirdre each name places she's been. Places like Crown Casino, Melbourne Town Hall, Docklands' New Year's Eve party, Federation Square on New Year's Day, the Melbourne Grand Prix, the MCG, and the new Melbourne Museum.

'At Melbourne's Entertainment Centre she "escorted" singer Kamahl to his spot on stage. She does charity work, and has entertained at a five-year-old's birthday party, as well as a fifty-year-old's birthday party,' says Deirdre. 'We currently do about one trip a month to Melbourne for some event or another with her. She's even appeared at "Bollywood burlesque" theme nights and at corporate awards nights. I need to get on the phone before every booking and ask people "Can you be the rear legs of Linda next weekend?" and so on.'

'We made something out of a joke,' says Ray.

It just goes to prove that their attitude towards being professional artists and having a go really works.

And so it was time for me to take some photographs as we tour their home and studio full of art and artifacts they've created. The sun still streams in through the unfinished section above a stairway. 'We must finish that this year,' Deirdre emphasises to Ray with *that* look. I know what *that* look means – my own wife has given me that same one mid-renovation.

Finally with photos complete and a last pat of the dogs, I'm off, leaving them to the rest of their day, and I wind my way through the mallee bush back to the main road. I know some things for sure: I will see their work again somewhere, and Ray and Deirdre are truly dedicated to their art and their lifestyle. And they sure as hell can make something out of nothing.

Charcoal Burner

NORMA BERRY
'PAY DAYS WERE GOOD – SANDWICHES AND BEER.
THE REST I'VE BEEN TRYING TO FORGET FOR YEARS.'

Next time you throw some charcoal in your backyard barbe-
cue, just remember it is people like Norma Berry who make
the charcoal and bag it. She was responsible for operating the
largest charcoal-producing company in Australia at Mathoura,
New South Wales, not far from the Murray River. She gave it
away in the mid-1990s and has been 'trying to forget about it
ever since,' so she says with a laugh. 'It was hot, filthy work.
The good old days: the dirt, the heat, the dust, smoke in the eyes
until they watered. Sometimes it was so thick you couldn't find
your way out of it. But I did love being out in the bush – the
birds singing, the gum trees. It was a job, good mates and not
too many blues.'

The first recorded charcoal burning dates back many centuries, and is an art in itself. Burn the wood too fast and for too

long and you end up with a useless pile of wood-ash. Burn it too slow and you end up with a pile of half-burnt logs.

All these things I was very keen to learn about. I had heard about Norma Berry in 2004, but it wasn't until 2007 that I finally got time to track her down and visit her on the property she shares with her soul-mate, Geoff Hammet. The property fronts the Gulpa Creek, near the station of the same name, but for some reason it's spelt differently – Gulpha Station is one of the old properties along the creek and isn't far from the Murray River.

I arrived at their farm on a warm day in February as I was en route to the outback. The shade of lovely trees surrounding the house was a relief from the sun, and I was greeted by the barking of two little dogs – Buddy, the fourteen-year-old bitzer, who came from an Echuca pet shop, and Will, the lively eight-month-old fox terrier-Jack Russell cross.

Norma said she didn't think she'd have much to tell me, but what she didn't know was that I really wanted to know all about charcoal burning. As a kid, I remember charcoal kilns not far from where I grew up, but they were long abandoned even then. We had eucalyptus factory kilns in the bush around town, as Inglewood, Victoria was the heart of the blue eucy oil industry. I grew up with eucalyptus oil coursing through my veins and lungs. One of nature's grandest smells – Australia's first export to the world – and I still use eucy oil.

Norma makes a cuppa tea and we sit at the kitchen table while the two dogs come to me for a pat. Then little Will decides it's time to chew some electrical wiring on a lamp. Geoff goes off to rescue it from the playful pup. Like Norma, Geoff also worked in the charcoal business – Norma was his boss. Soon, they enlightened me on how they went about making charcoal, but first I wanted to learn more of their lives. Norma told me all about hers.

'Well, I was born at Cohuna in 1940. When Dad came home from the army we moved to Moama to start a poultry farm. After Dad left, Mum, my sister Joan and I moved from the Riverina poultry farm into Echuca, where we went to high school. Years later I ended up married with five kids – all girls. I'd worked in a jewellers shop, a bakers, and Moran & Cato Grocers, and ended up alone as I separated from my husband. I met Colin Leech, a charcoal burner – an old bushie bloke – who worked with timber, logs, firewood and charcoal on a property called Longreach, a property owned by the Arthur family from Moulamein. So I started work with him. He was a rough and tough old bloke. A couple of years later we moved the charcoal business to Mathoura on Tocumwal Road on the banks of the Edward River. It was the late seventies or the early eighties, I think.'

Norma isn't good with dates. Geoff isn't good with dates. So we had some fun working out a time frame. Clippings from various newspapers and magazines helped.

'Old Colin Leech ended up pretty sick with arthritis and emphysema, and one day he asked me to take it on, take over the business from him. So I did. I'd go out early each morning, put the fire on and boil the kettle. The business had about thirty large steel kilns, which were basically boxes made from heavy-duty steel. I had the worst job out there, lighting the first kiln and controlling the burn. You had to put a corrugated iron sheet roof on top of the boxes. The smoke was unbelievable.

'Later we also had about six railway carriages to use as kilns as well. At best, we had nineteen employees, but usually only about ten to twelve employees. Over the years we had a lot of

Aboriginal workers from Deniliquin or Echuca. The business supplied all the charcoal to Barbeques Galore in Sydney, who then distributed all over Australia.'

Norma didn't know that I had been told by a former forestry officer that the owner of the business had had a hard time. 'Norma, though, was a great worker and could keep them in line,' he said.

'Workers had to be jacks-of-all-trades,' said Norma. 'They had to have their chainsaw licences and a fork lift, etc. While some stacked five or six kilns, there would be another five or six kilns burning, and another five or six kilns being emptied of charcoal, and workers would load the charcoal into bags. We bagged 4.5-kilo bags and stapled them up, and 20-kilo bags were sewn. A couple of women helped with the smaller bags. In those days a 20-kilo bag cost $7 retail and it was $2 for a 4.5-kilo bag. One kiln would produce twenty-five to thirty of the big bags. It would take 5 or 6 tonnes of tightly packed wood to make 1 tonne of charcoal in one kiln.

'We sent some charcoal to a distributor in Melbourne who supplied wood-fired cafés and pizza places. Once a week, Kevin Wilson Transport of Elmore took a semi-load of charcoal to Sydney. He carried 1000 big bags and 6000 little bags every trip. Once a week. The small bags were loaded on to pallets. Some also went to Tasmania from Melbourne, but Barbeques Galore had all theirs sent to Sydney and they distributed Australia-wide themselves. Most of the loading onto trucks in those days was done by hand: heavy, dirty work. It was all done in pairs – two blokes on the truck stacking, two blokes carrying and loading off the ground. Hard bloody yakka.'

While in his day Colin Leech ran the business for about five years, it was Norma who kept it going for fifteen years until

1995. 'Colin was tough, he was always yelling out "You useless bastard!" at someone. Colin Leech died four years ago,' said Norma. I asked if many of the locals worked there. Both Geoff and Norma continue to compare notes and test their memories. They both threw some names at me.

'We had many workers come and go over the years,' said Norma. Geoff rattled off some names – Skinny, Jack Barnes, Boondie, Yogie, Kenny Smith, Herbie, David Murray, Hector, Robin Doolan, Oink, Hat, Bugs, Gearbox, Old Jim, Jamie, Hoggie. Great Aussie nicknames. Both he and Norma said their memories had slipped.

Mathoura Charcoal was a good business and many, many Australians would have used the charcoal having no idea where it came from or how it was made. It was an all-Aussie bush business.

'In those days,' said Geoff, 'there were no roll bars, no helmets, no safety equipment. We had numerous hazards – truck and machinery breakdowns, total fire ban days, fires, floods. No bushfires were ever started from the charcoal plant though.'

'And we still had to pay the Forestry Commission royalties regardless,' says Norma. 'The total fire ban days were the worst. They don't run out until midnight, so I'd have to go out there on my own and light up after midnight. I lit nineteen kilns one night on my own, put the roofs on, inserted all the breather pipes (eight to each kiln) and sealed all the kilns. It was a long night. When floods came we'd have to stop. We'd get bogged in the forests, and all that,' she says.

'In winter time the dogs would all sleep so close to the kilns for warmth they'd singe and burn their fur. About three times a year they'd bring tourist buses into the bush to see us work and I'd explain the whole process.'

'It was a big job,' says Geoff. 'Not everyone could do it; you had to have a knack for it. Norma was good. She always did the lighting up.'

'It is important to get it right,' Norma adds. 'When a kiln was tightly stacked you had 2-inch breather pipes underneath the load of wood. They went into the load about 18 inches. When I lit a stack up, you then had to get it burning really well for twenty-four hours, and the secret was in the sealing up of the kilns with wet sand and heavy mud until it was airtight, and then taking the pipes out. Twenty-four hours of burning. Once I lit the first kiln, I could then take shovel loads of ash and move to start the fires on the next kiln and so on.

'I was always a tomboy and always enjoyed the bush,' she says. 'I was a chainsaw champion and had my own saw, still have it,' says Norma matter-of-factly. 'I won the Championship Chainsaw event about six to eight years in a row at Mathoura. I won my section in the under 80 cc class six years in a row, then they put me up into the big open-class. The event was you stood beside a huge log, cut off a slice of log downwards, and then one slice coming from the bottom of the log upwards. I was the only female in the fastest chainsaw competition, and they were not impressed when I won it,' laughs Norma. 'I beat some of my own blokes who worked for Mathoura Charcoal and others in the championships, which didn't go down too well with a couple of them.'

I asked if she still competed, but because the event is no longer held she doesn't. 'But I probably would have to have a go still if they had it,' she says with a smile. A nice engraved silver tray was just one of the trophies she won over the years. I asked if she was trained. 'Nah, I was just self-taught.'

I didn't ask Geoff if he had competed, but he did seem pretty pleased with his mate. He showed me the photograph of the silver tray trophy she had won.

Geoff worked at the kilns for a number of years, and like Norma was able to give me good information as well. Wood of all sorts, mainly off-cuts about 18 inches thick, and a lot of smaller stuff was collected in the forests. The more they could get tightly packed into a kiln, the more they would get out as charcoal. There was no felling of trees in the forests; they followed the timber contractors and cleaned up after them, using what would have normally been left as rubbish to rot, or burn. They stacked the lengths of timber tightly as they went. A usual stack in the kilns was about 10 feet long by 6 feet wide and 6 feet high, and made up of solid timber of all sorts. The heavy-gauge steel in the tanks or kilns was specially made. Some they picked up from another charcoal burner. It would take a full week to finish a turnover of kilns. While mud and sand sealed them, the heat was so intense it took a week for them to cool down.

I sensed Geoff was a real bushie also, and so while Norma made another cuppa and attended to something outside, we talked of his life. 'I was only out there for about two years. I was born at Nyah West in 1955, but grew up at Boundary Bend on the Murray River. I went to Robinvale High School and worked on my father's place – cattle and oranges – on the Murray Valley Highway, when it was gravel road and we had no power. Later I picked peas, carrots, grapes, dried fruit sultanas. I still hate carrots. Then I went to a place near Jerilderie where I worked as a jackaroo for three years. Then I had wanderlust – worked as a painter and docker at the Whyalla Shipyards, and did plumbing in Stratco, Geelong, then worked

on the building of the Thompson River Dam in Gippsland, and then Shepparton, building labs for the Tatura Research Institute for three years. After that I spent some time doing general farm work on crops. I was married in 1978, had Brooke in 1981, and Scott in 1982. I was in Mathoura in 1981. My wife and I split up. I worked here on Gulpha Station, doing general farm work, and bought 120 acres of it as my own farm and have been here ever since, some twenty-five years. Here I've had cattle, sheep, watermelons, spuds and other veggies. I also have had a sleeper-cutting mill on the Murrumbidgee River for three and a half years.'

But as I had driven in the front gate and made my way down the duty track to the oasis house under the big old trees, I couldn't help but notice that the property is up for sale. I asked Geoff about it. 'Yep,' he says, 'we're looking at buying a big bus. We've looked at a couple already. But we have to sell first, and with this drought, who will buy it in a hurry? So we'll just wait and see.'

Norma adds, 'Then we are off to travel Australia with two dogs, three goldfish and eight or nine little tacker fish called zebras. We'll have to sell our six chooks, rooster and ducks.'

I was left with no doubt that they really are looking forward to their big adventure and full time life on the road. I reckon they will be able to turn their hands to anything. Getting stuck into it doesn't seem a worry to these people.

And so it was time for me to do likewise, go follow that blue-tar ribbon heading north. I was heading to Hay, Booligal and beyond, across the wide open plains. I had a date with shearing contractors in a big shearing shed and it was mid-afternoon. It would still take another day and a half to get there.

We took some photos in the backyard, and I got to pat my little mate Will again before I was off and back on the bitumen. Sounds like a good title for a book. It suits my lifestyle – *Back on the Bitumen*. I spend a lot of time on it and off it in search of the great bush Aussies such as Geoff, and the lady they know as Norma the chainsaw champion – and charcoal burner.

Whipstick

PETER WORTHINGTON

'POETRY HELPS KEEP OUR HERITAGE ALIVE; IT TEACHES THE YOUNG
ABOUT THE BUSH AND HOW OUR COUNTRY WAS MADE.'

I first met him at a friend's place years ago, and again, briefly, at the Melbourne Show ute competition. Then I met him at home about ten days after he had his second heart turn. He had recovered well. But then a further bunch of heart attacks laid him low.

Now finally I get to tell his story.

Peter Worthington was born in Melbourne in 1945 and moved to Robinvale when he was about four. His father originally came from over the river at Euston, New South Wales. Peter spent his school years there, but was not really a fan of school.

'I was "invited" to leave school when I was thirteen and a half years old, then in later years I did night school. Much of my school English papers were filled in with poetry.'

His first job was as a counter assistant at Cox Brothers Australia in Robinvale. He says then he was laid off in 'Prime Minister Bob Menzies' credit squeeze' in 1960.

'I then started my apprenticeship with my father, my grandfather and Dad's three brothers. They were all bricklayers. The first of my ancestors came from England in 1886 – many generations of brickies in the family. I still have my tuck-pointing tools.

'Whenever I had a fight with my father or grandfather or any of them, I'd go bush, where I did all sorts of work like truck driving, boundary riding, fencing, mustering, roo shooting, well cleaning, rabbit trapping. Just general bush skills. Tried shearing but I hated it, worse on the back than bricklaying. I used to travel to the far western parts of New South Wales – places like Innamincka, Birdsville, Ivanhoe, Hillston, Balranald, Maude and places like that. Did it for six years on and off.

'In 1965 I did national service (also called the nashos). I was already a Corporal in CMF (Army Reserve) when I was conscripted. After I joined, I was sent back to home camp in Mildura to do recruitment training, then later to Kapooka at Wagga, also in recruit training. With both the CMF and the nashos I ended up doing nine years. Then in 1967 I was accepted as a trainee linesman with the Post Master General in Golden Square. I ended up in country primary work, doing trunk cable installation and set ups all over the place. Then I ended up as a technical instructor in the Golden Square Telecom School until I was made redundant with many others in 1988.

'Later I was self-employed for a number of years doing sheds, concrete work, steel fabrication, building chook sheds and all that sort of stuff. My first marriage came to an end after eighteen years, and I have three kids – Megan is thirty-five, Ryan is thirty-three, and Clare is twenty-nine.'

Peter managed a trout farm for about six months, and later was part of a company that dismantled and recycled car parts. He and his second wife of thirteen years have a daughter, Sharni, who is seventeen.

'I spent eighteen years as a State Emergency Service volunteer and was awarded a national medal for service to the community,' he says. 'Then between 1993 and 1999 I worked with a training company with unemployed youth and street kids doing training, and I was also a safety officer. I'm now fully retired. Well, sort of.'

It is here that the character of Whipstick takes over from Peter. Whipstick is a character who recites poetry, mainly the humorous kind, but now he's looking at changing his style – to a softer type.

'I first started in 1996: I gave a pub performance. Both my grandfather and mother wrote poetry. I was in bed crook and I wrote "Billy Russell's Revenge", and have written a couple of hundred since then. At the Raywood Hotel I used to write a poem to be read out each Friday called "Wally of the Week", and it would be a ditty about one of the drinkers in the pub. I did that for about three years.

'I come from a fairly musical family, but I didn't play music. My mother said, "Don't try and sing." She reckoned I always had a voice for poetry. I've always liked Australian bush poetry – Henry Lawson, 'Banjo' Paterson, Barcroft Boake, George Essex Evans, Father John O'Brien. I also like Duke Tritton, who at eighteen went bush for eight years and tramped around. He wrote "Shearing in the Bar" near Dunlop Station in New South Wales. Henry Lawson is probably the best. He

293

told it from the real side of life. Paterson was good, too, but different.

'I recite some of Paterson's works, like "Mulga Bill's Bicycle", "The Man from Ironbark" and "Clancy of the Overflow", and such, but I'm only now learning some of Lawson's stuff for a new show.

'My aim in reciting Australian poetry is to help keep our heritage alive; it teaches the young about the bush and how our country was made. There are four styles of poetry, I reckon. Traditional old master stuff; modern, which is twentieth century; our own original written works; and what I call "ratbag poems". In my two-hour show I do about 70 per cent of my own original works and about 30 per cent of other people's work.'

In 1999 Peter self-published some of his poems in a small book titled *Fiddlestick, a collection of yarns and verse by Whipstick Wortho*. The twenty-two poems include one called 'The Stockman's Lament'. It was written by his grandfather P.J. (Jack) O'Shannessy (1888–1951) some time in the 1920s. But I've chosen one of Wortho's own poems for you to ponder over.

KNOCKIN' DOWN THE GUN

Me old mate Slim was drinking,
Up the pub, the other day.
You can find him there most nights,
He reckons, it helps to pass the time away.

As always happy and smiling,
A real top kind of bloke.
But this night he upset a smart alec,
And made him the butt of his joke.

It started with a young shearer,
Who claimed he was a gun.
As Slim listened to his stories,
He thought he would have some fun.

He said, 'Where have you shorn boy?'
The gun said, 'All over New South Wales.'
And the more the young bloke said,
The taller become his tales.

Now as his bulldust ebbed and flowed,
Slim just sat there, a smile all over his face.
He said, 'What was your record boy?
And what was the name of the place?'

'It was a station called Koonawarra,
That was the first shed that I rung,
We were shearin' fine wool merinos,
And I done eighty on every run.'

Slim said, 'What, three hundred and twenty a day?
That's a good job for a lad.'
But with Slim's next statement,
It left the gun looking a bit mad.

He said, 'It was way back in fifty-eight,
That's when I hit the news.
We were shearing border leicesters,
And I shore four hundred and thirty ewes.'

The gun with a look of hate,
Stood up and then he spat.
'In what flamin' shed?' he said,
'Did you do bloody that?'

> Now Slim just gave a smile,
> With wrinkles on his brow.
> He said, 'Son, it was right on that barstool
> Where you have been shearing now.'

The same year as he released his book, he took out a Judge's Highly Commended trophy at the 1999 Australian Bush Poetry Championships.

Whipstick has appeared at schools in many towns. At one school he also showed students about cooking in a camp oven. 'I've cooked in camp ovens back as far as I can remember. My father was a good bushman and taught all us six sons and a daughter to survive in any climate.'

Peter has also performed at pubs, clubs, community halls, weddings, bucks parties, cafés and festivals. The festivals include performances at the Tamworth Country Music Festival, the Mildura Country Music Festival and the Corryong Man from Snowy River Festival, and he is now one of the judges at Corryong. He says he has worked in nineteen towns over Victoria and New South Wales.

'I'm wherever they want me whenever, if the money is right and fair.'

This was where Whipstick's story sat for a long time. I had notes that became out of date as he moved. We lost contact for a while and then the heart attacks meant he wasn't up to writing or performing, or probably being bothered by a wandering author. Whipstick has had a total of eight heart attacks, but we finally got to chat and he was a happy man.

'I've since had four major heart operations. The last one, my lady – who is a nurse – told me that I was having a heart attack, and I said that I wasn't as it felt different, but she wouldn't take no for an answer and whipped me off to hospital. Twenty minutes later I was being flown to Melbourne for an operation. They said I died twice, but they got me going again. She saved my life, really.'

That lady is Kerry, and she now shares life with Whipstick, and they are both happy people. Both have had some tough knocks, but now they own a new home near the beach and Kerry has just changed to a new nursing job, and they walk on the beach every day of their lives.

'I love it. It is absolute heaven. I knew Kerry about thirty-five years ago in the bush, and then I ran into her as she owned a café near where I was living in the bush. One of my daughters and one of her sons went to school together.

'Anyway, now we are beach people and we're loving it. We live 800 yards' walk from the bay in one direction, or five minutes in the car, and I'm at a back beach where I do a bit of surf fishing. I have a little boat, and on good days I go and catch some flathead and some whiting, which is different for a bloke who is used to fishing the Murray all the time. Life is like that, it changes and you make the best of it. Always take every opportunity and look for the good things and be positive.

'I've got a goal to be the first Worthington male to live past seventy. They all died young – Dad was only sixty-five. Heart attacks run in the family. Uncle Bill and Bert and Aunt Jess all died young, too. Cancer took my mum, and others in the family have had cancer too. I'm sixty-two now so I have a few years to go, but I plan to make it okay.'

Before he left the bush, Whipstick was starting to get back into appearing at places, performing his poetry and yarns. 'I was asked to do an elderly citizens gig, and they said to come dressed up, so no one knows you. There were about seventy

people in the audience who knew me, but I surprised everyone by turning up dressed as Santa with no hair or beard, as I had shaved the lot off. I said, "I'm Whipstick's younger brother, Bob," and no one guessed it was really me. I did half an hour of poems and stuff and was having a cuppa tea with the old dears. One lady came up and said to me, "You look and sound a lot like your brother." I said, "Well, you should know, we were in the rehabilitation pool together yesterday." She said, "What do you mean?" Everyone got a shock when I replied, "I'm Peter, not Bob. I just shaved my beard and hair off to surprise you lot." We all had a bit of a laugh. The hair and beard are back now, but not as long as before.'

Nowadays, Whipstick and Kerry enjoy the good life. Whipstick has a new lease of life and says Kerry is a real soul-mate. He spends time doing a bit of gardening and does a couple of lawns to pick up a few bob.

When he was lying in hospital recovering he knew that his writing days were still not over, and it gave him an opportunity to reflect on life and how lucky he has been. One nurse told him that he looked a bit stressed, so he asked for a pen and piece of paper and before long 'Whipstick's Ghost' was written. Some of his writing includes his thoughts on life in rehabilitation. One was called 'Get on With it', which is about getting on with life after trauma. In order to lose a bit of weight and get fit again, he took on delivering junk mail; 'Disgrunted Junk Mailer' was the result. 'Women are amazing; they chase you up and demand their junk mail. What they don't know is it is usually their husbands who have thrown it in the bin. Some people can't live without junk mail; others absolutely hate you for delivering it and tell you so. You can't win, so I wrote the poem to suit. Since I now have to watch what I eat, I've seen how hard it is in supermarkets, and so I wrote 'The Panel', which describes what is in food. The food labels in supermarkets are amazing, and inspired me to write it.

'Recently I was asked to do a live gig in a street parade, and the next day a lady come up to me in the street and asked if I'd do the local nursing home. I did all the 'Banjo' Paterson stuff – the oldies love it. From there I was asked to do a charity show at the boat ramp, raising money for local charity. So as you can see I'm still doing it, and writing again makes me feel really good.'

There is no doubt Peter plans to be around for a lot longer, and he's doing the right things to make sure. He has a positive attitude and his writing is an outlet that he has used for many years, and it has brought a laugh to many people over the years.

Long may he keep pushing that pen.

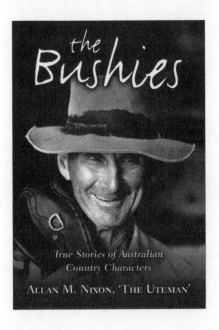

The Bushies

ALLAN M. NIXON

The Bushies offers a rare glimpse of country Australia through stories of real Australians - both ordinary and extraordinary. 'The Uteman', Allan M. Nixon, travelled far and wide to find this dinkum cross-section of bush identities. One of them, a missing person for nearly three decades, was reunited with his family as a result and in 2004 was featured on the ABC's television program *Australian Story*.

A banjo maker, a modern gold miner, a legendary artist and treehouse-dweller. And many more . . . Individual, irrepressible and usually irreverent, they are *The Bushies*.

Subscribe to receive *read more*, your monthly newsletter from Penguin Australia. As a *read more* subscriber you'll receive sneak peeks of new books, be kept up to date with what's hot, have the opportunity to meet your favourite authors, download reading guides for your book club, receive special offers, be in the running to win exclusive subscriber-only prizes, plus much more.

Visit penguin.com.au to subscribe.